COMPREHENSIVE
COMBAT FITNESS TRAINING

**PROGRAM DESIGN FOR CIVILIANS,
LAW ENFORCEMENT AND MILITARY**

> **WARNING:** *Do not start any fitness program without first consulting a qualified physician. In addition, some of the more advanced techniques in this book can be dangerous if performed incorrectly and we encourage you to consult a certified personal trainer or physical therapist to ensure you are using proper form. Whenever conducting climbing activities, be sure to observe proper safety procedures and use all necessary handholds, spotters and safety equipment.*

Special Tactics, LLC

Special Tactics and the Special Tactics Logo are registered trademarks of Special Tactics, LLC

© 2017 by Special Tactics, LLC

ISBN 978-1-945137-10-5

Except as permitted under U.S. Copyright Law, no part of this book may be reprinted, reproduced, transmitted, or utilized in any form by any electronic, mechanical, or other means, now known or hereafter invented, including photocopying, microfilming, and recording, or in any information storage or retrieval system, without written permission from Special Tactics, LLC.

Contents

COMBAT FITNESS: A Mission Focused Approach 7
    A Mission Focused Approach   8

PERFORMANCE EVALUATION: For Mission Focused Training 11
    Example 1: The Ideal   11
    Example 2: Low-Budget Law Enforcement Option   12
    Example 3: Low-Budget Military Option   13
    Evaluation Design Process   13

EXERCISE & TRAINING TECHNIQUES

Mobility Training 21
    Running Form   22
    Running Drills   30
    Running Workouts   38
    Speed/Agility Ladder   41
    Power Plyometrics   42
    Speed Plyometrics   50
    Cross-Country Movement and Rucking   52
    Obstacle Course Training   54
    Climbing, Swimming and Water Survival   55

Strength Training 57
    Core Strength Exercises   58
    Body Weight Exercises   62
    Free Weight Exercises   64
    Cable Exercises   76

Balance, Coordination and Dexterity 83

Stick Training 84
Sports Training 95
Other Balance and Coordination Drills 96
Hand and Grip Training 97

Flexibility, Recovery and Nutrition 99

Flexibility 100
Recovery 107
Nutrition 111

PROGRAM DESIGN AND TRACKING

Workout and Fitness Program Design 119

Workout Scheduling: Workout Time Blocks 120
Workout Scheduling: Weekly Routines 121
Workout Scheduling: Periodization 122
Fitness Program Design: Integrating Different Types of Workouts 123
Fitness Program Design: The Special Tactics Approach 125
Fitness Program Design Examples 129

Performance Tracking Techniques 141

Performance Tracking Fundamentals 141
Fitness Testing and Combat Performance Evaluations 143
Program Modification and Optimization 144

CONCLUSION: A Habit of Adaptation 147

To those who have gone before us, the living and the fallen

COMBAT FITNESS
A Mission Focused Approach

Many fitness books and courses focus on a specific set of exercises or techniques and suggest that a single fitness system is superior to all others. It is impossible to know if such claims are correct or incorrect. However, this book suggests that the "best" fitness system for you can vary dramatically based on your personal requirements and individual physical characteristics. Your personality, preferences and mindset can also affect which fitness system is the best fit for you.

Therefore, the purpose of this book is not to provide you with a fixed set of exercises to perform or a rigid fitness program to follow. It is likely that you already have a fitness program and have chosen exercises and routines that work for you. If this is the case, the purpose of this book is to provide concepts and ideas that can help you to optimize and possibly improve your existing program. If you do not currently have a fitness program, this book can help you develop one that fits your individual needs.

While the focus of this book is not exercises and techniques, it would be impossible to discuss fitness or performance enhancement without a set of techniques to use as a reference or baseline. Therefore, a large portion of this book does discuss a variety of exercise techniques and explains how to perform them. These techniques serve only as examples and you can apply the principles outlined in this book and incorporate your own preferred techniques. So, once again we caution the reader not to get wrapped up in the techniques described in this book but instead focus on the more important, higher-level principles of combat fitness performance enhancement that are so frequently overlooked by programs that focus too much on specific techniques.

That being said, you may find some of the techniques in this book useful and decide to incorporate them into your own fitness program. We selected the techniques in this book based on three criteria. First, we wanted to select a wide variety of techniques drawing from many different fitness systems and disciplines. Second, we included techniques that were either less known, or frequently performed incorrectly, in an attempt to provide readers with something new that they might not find in other books. Finally, we chose techniques that can prove useful and functional for the combat athlete in a variety of mission sets.

A Mission Focused Approach

As just mentioned, many debates on tactical fitness focus on the question of which exercises or routines are the most effective. We believe this is the wrong question to be asking. The more important question is, how do we measure whether a fitness program actually improves effectiveness in a given mission set? After all, the ultimate goal is not to improve your fitness or appearance, but to maximize your chances of winning the next combat engagement and increase your chances of surviving the worst-case scenario. It is not always easy to determine whether or not a fitness program will contribute to mission success. The following five steps provide a good starting point for developing a mission focused fitness program.

1) Develop a Combat Performance Evaluation - The essential first step in building every aspect of your training program, including the fitness routine, is developing a combat performance evaluation. Most military performance evaluations test only one attribute at a time (marksmanship, fitness, casualty care) in an isolated environment. A combat performance evaluation tests multiple skills/attributes simultaneously under realistic conditions with little or no warning provided to those being evaluated. The following are some suggestions for developing a good combat performance evaluation:

- *Replicate realistic mission/combat scenarios as closely as possible.*
- *Test multiple combat skills/ attributes in a single evaluation.*
- *Those evaluated should never know what to expect on the test.*
- *Evaluations do not have to be long, complicated, labor-intensive or expensive.*
- *Try to conduct at least one short and simple evaluation each week.*
- *Record the results (preferably with video) to track progress over time.*

2) Deveop a Fitness Program Based on Evaluation Results - Performance failures in the evaluation will highlight fitness deficiencies that are affecting mission performance. Are team members having trouble shooting accurately because they are out of breath? Are team members not strong enough to drag casualties or climb walls in their gear? The combat performance evaluation helps you develop a fitness program that fits your specific mission requirements. No single fitness program is the right fit for all tactical units. For example, if you are in a military long-range reconnaissance unit, it is probably not in your interest (or in the interest of your teammates who might have to carry you) to focus on weight training and increasing body mass. Conversely, cross-country mobility is not as important for a tactical team tasked with controlling prison riots. Subduing angry inmates (who spend most of their time lifting weights) requires maximum body mass, explosive strength and speed. The program must fit the mission.

3) Develop Metrics to Measure and Track Physical Performance - Once you determine which physical attributes and exercises are most critical to mission success, you then must track your rate of improvement in those attributes and exercises. Even dedicated athletes often forget to track their performance. How is it possible to know if a fitness program is truly working if you are not aware of how changes in the program affect the rate of progress? While it can be tedious, it is critical to record your performance in every physical exercise and track progress over time. Ideally, you should then make minor adjustments to the routine, nutrition and recovery to measure whether these changes increase or decrease the rate of performance improvement. This will help you optimize the program design.

4) Adjust the Program Based on Individual Body Type and Personal Preference - Even if all members of a unit share the same mission requirements, this does not mean that they must share the exact same fitness routine. Everyone's body is different. A program that works for one person may not work for someone else. Therefore, while remaining aware of mission requirements, use the program that is the best fit for you, physically and mentally. It is fine to incorporate existing commercial routines, athletic routines or military routines that have worked for you in the past, as long as your combat performance evaluation results are improving.

5) Focus on Preparing for the Worst-Case Scenario - One critical factor in combat fitness training is that combat fitness often proves most important in the "worst-case scenario." A direct-action assault unit might not expect to conduct a grueling escape and evasion across the desert. However, their ability to do so might mean the difference between life and death should things go wrong on their mission. Therefore, in developing combat performance evaluations, it is wise to incorporate unexpected setbacks and simulated worst-case scenarios.

Following the five steps above is the general framework for developing a mission focused combat fitness program. The remainder of this book will provide more detail on how to complete each of the five steps, while offering suggestions and examples of possible routines tailored for different mission sets. It is important to remember that all of the concepts, processes and techniques explained in this book are meant to serve only as guidelines and it is best to adjust them based on your own individual or unit requirements.

COMBAT PERFORMANCE EVALUATION
For Mission Focused Training

The first critical step in the mission focused approach is to develop a combat performance evaluation that replicates the mission requirements you are likely to face in real life. As already mentioned, most performance evaluations in military and law enforcement units test only one skill/attribute at a time (marksmanship, fitness, casualty care) in an isolated environment. An effective combat performance evaluation tests multiple skills/attributes simultaneously under realistic conditions, with little or no warning provided to those being evaluated. What follows are a few examples of how to design and implement a combat performance evaluation.

Example 1: The Ideal

This is an example of how you might design a combat performance evaluation if your organization has unlimited resources and no external restrictions. We understand that this is rarely the case, but it is still useful to have a picture of the ideal scenario as a reference point to strive for when operating under organizational constraints. In addition, should threat levels increase, organizational constraints may fade away and more resources might become available to tactical units, allowing for more realistic and resource-intensive combat performance evaluations.

The less warning your people have the better. You might have an alarm in your facility/compound to signal the start of the test. You might have different codes or alarms to allow you to test only select groups at a time. Once the alarm goes off, those being tested must drop what they are doing, don their combat equipment and move as quickly as possible to a predetermined rally point. Once they arrive, the tester will reveal the first event. For example, the tester might point to a casualty or dummy and tell the group that they must treat the casualty, move the casualty to a helicopter landing zone and call for evacuation. Ideally, the test will include live fire or non-lethal weapons engagements, forcing the group to seek cover, identify and engage targets while they are dealing with the casualty.

The tester should unexpectedly introduce changes into the scenario, testing different skills and making the events as physically demanding as possible. The group might have to move the casualty upstairs, send a radio message from the roof, but then lower the casualty out of a window using a rope system because the lower floors of the building catch fire. The amount of stress you can induce is limited only by your goals for the evaluation and the skill of your people. It is important to remember that skills testing should not get in the way of fitness testing. You should intersperse physical challenges (like climbing, sprinting and negotiating obstacles) between the skills tests so that your people never get to recover completely.

Example 2: Low-Budget Law Enforcement Option

Even without the resources and freedom of action described in the previous example, you can still design an effective combat performance evaluation with very few resources. You will still use the same basic principles and structure from the ideal example, you will just have to be more resourceful.

You will use the same surprise alert method. Officers must don their equipment and move to a rally point, maybe the top floor of your office building. Once there, they will receive instructions for their first event. For example, they must run down to the bottom floor to another rally point where they find a heavy bag of equipment that they must carry back up to the top floor. Once on the top floor they open the bag to find a mass of disassembled weapons, radios and other equipment that they must reassemble as quickly as possible.

Once complete, they are instructed to take the equipment with them and move as quickly as possible to the parking lot where they are told to get into their car and drive to an emergency call. When they arrive in the parking lot they are told that they are taking fire from a heavily armed active shooter (deadly attacker) on the opposite side of the garage. While there will be no live-fire shooting, you can use speakers to replicate the sound of gunfire and increase stress. The attacker will be a role-player and the officers must take cover and use the radio to report the attacker's description and location. From here, you might incorporate a casualty scenario where the officers must drag a casualty to safety, report status and provide medical aid.

For the next event, you might report that the attacker has fled to the gym or a room where you have set up grappling mats. The officers might have to run up and down stairs (or sprint across the parking lot) two more times and then enter the room to arrest the subject. The officers must use verbal commands and physical contact to control the subject but then another attacker will emerge unexpectedly and both officers will need to use defensive tactics/combatives (in a safe manner) to control and restrain both attackers.

Once again, this is just an example and there is no limit to how creative you can be when designing scenarios. You can choose to have the officers run through the course individually, with a partner, or as a larger team. It is important to focus on skills and abilities that are most relevant to your mission requirements. For example, park police in a rural area might want to incorporate longer movements, simulating pursuit of a suspect over wooded or rough terrain.

Example 3: Low-Budget Military Option

A low-budget military version of the test would look very similar to the previous example but the skill and fitness focus would be different. A military unit might include tasks like map reading and cross-country navigation, or moving as quickly as possible carrying a crew-served weapon and then putting that weapon into operation. A military test might also incorporate maintenance tasks like changing a tire or track on an armored vehicle. Other useful evaluation tasks might include casualty evacuation/care, calling for artillery/air support and emergency rope operations. Tests can be short and intense, or they can also last much longer, running for several hours or even days. It all depends on your mission requirements.

Evaluation Design Process

The examples above should give you a clearer understanding of the nature of the combat performance evaluation. However, it is unlikely that any of the examples above will be a perfect fit for you or your organization. Instead, you must take deliberate steps to identify your mission requirements and design your combat performance evaluation accordingly.

STEP 1: Develop Initial Demands List Using Historical Data

The most useful source of information about your mission requirements can be found in your own organizational records and reports. If you are part of a law enforcement unit, what kind of real-life challenges (particularly physical challenges) has your unit faced over the past two or three years? If you are part of a military unit, what were the main challenges your unit encountered during your last combat deployment? Some of this data might be available in mission reports, but you should also question key leaders and experienced individuals to get their perspectives.

It is generally best to assign a single individual to lead the development of the combat performance evaluation. This individual should carefully review combat reports, organizational records and interview key personnel as needed. The goal is to compile a list of physical, mental and skill-related demands on real-world operations. If there is a lack of available data in your unit, you may want to draw data from other units that share a similar mission or operational environment. It may also be useful to review historical records from past conflicts or from other countries. For example, when developing a physical training regimen for jungle warfare, your unit might not have much data on the demands of jungle combat. You might need to review after action reports from the Vietnam War or reach out to contacts in allied nations that engage in jungle warfare more regularly.

Whatever sources you use to develop the demands list, the initial list does not have to be perfect. There is only so much you can do with historical data and external input. The purpose of the list is to provide a starting point for the subsequent discussions where the unit will come together to work out a more complete list that accounts for future requirements as well as past experiences. Therefore, it is always better to include more items on the initial demands list since items can always be removed or modified later on.

STEP 2: Refine the Demands List Using Group Discussion

Once you have accomplished as much as possible using historical data and outside research, the next step is to present the initial list to the unit as a whole and have an open discussion to refine and modify the list. In smaller units, it may be useful to include every member of the unit in the discussion. In larger units, the discussion may include only key leaders and selected personnel. In general, the larger the discussion group is and the more willing individuals are to argue and present different opinions, the better the final product will be.

Some military units might have more formalized procedures for establishing a Mission Essential Task List (METL) and much of it might be directed by higher command. In theory, this METL could be used to establish a combat performance evaluation. However, units will often achieve better results with a "bottom up" approach to developing their own combat performance evaluation, as long as they are operating within the bounds of the directed METL and the higher commander's intent.

The individual in charge of developing the list of demands will present his/her results to the group as a starting point for the expanded list. The group will consider the items on the list and decide whether it is likely that the unit will encounter similar demands in the future or not. The moderator should then ask members of the group to offer suggestions of demands that should be added to the list. The group will continue to debate and refine the list until the majority of personnel agree that it is complete.

In many cases, the process will not need to be that complicated since the potential physical demands of future operations and combat engagements may be relatively straightforward. For example, for law enforcement patrol officers, key demands might include pursuing a suspect through urban terrain, negotiating obstacles like walls or ladders, engaging targets accurately in the vicinity of innocent civilians and dragging a casualty to safety. It might not require extensive historical research and group meetings to identify those demands. However, it is still useful to go through the motions of reviewing past operations and engaging in group discussion since the process might identify important demands that were not obvious on the surface.

STEP 3: Prioritize the Demands List

Once the group has agreed on the demands list, the next step is to prioritize the list based on which demands are the most likely and which are the most critical. The prioritization does not need to be perfect and there is no fixed formula for prioritizing the various physical demands. However, going through the motions of prioritizing the various physical demands is an important step in helping the organization think about the true nature of its operational and physical fitness requirements. The unit can always adjust the demands list or the priority order at any time based on new information and/or operational feedback.

STEP 4: Use the Demands List to Develop a Performance Evaluations Binder

Once the demands list is created, it leaves the group and returns to the individual responsible for developing the performance evaluations. Ideally, the exact content and nature of the performance evaluations should be kept secret as much as possible in order to ensure each evaluation is a surprise and unit members cannot "game" the test. If unit members know what to expect, the evaluation will not realistically represent combat conditions.

The evaluation developer will compile a bank of various combat performance evaluations to be used in the future. It is preferable to create several evaluations of varying duration and resource requirements. The best evaluations might be very long, involved and resource intensive. However, this will also mean that it will be difficult to execute those evaluations frequently enough to gather timely feedback and performance data. Therefore, there should also be shorter, simpler evaluations that are not as resource intensive that can be executed more frequently. It is ideal to conduct some sort of evaluation at least once per week and that could be very difficult to accomplish without designing simple, economical evaluation options.

The evaluation designer does not need to work alone. For larger units, it may be preferable to assign a small planning cell to design and run evaluations. Once again, the important point is that the majority of the unit being tested is not aware of the details of the evaluations. For this reason, the evaluation design process should remain contained within the cell. It may be useful to maintain binders that compile and categorize the various performance evaluations. This will allow the designers to add new evaluations to the binder over time, creating a diverse library of evaluations to choose from.

STEP 5: Establish an Evaluation Schedule

Once the evaluations binder is complete, the designers will coordinate with the unit leadership to establish a schedule for combat performance evaluations. In some cases, the leaders themselves might want to participate in the evaluations and will therefore prefer to not know all the details of each evaluation. In other cases, only the command element will have access to the schedule. Some units may choose to publish the schedule to all unit members but leave the details of individual evaluations a secret. It is up to each unit to establish its own preferences for how to ensure each evaluation is a surprise, while not disrupting the unit's administrative requirements or other important events.

Again, it is ideal to conduct some sort of evaluation once per week. If time and resources are limited, the more frequent evaluations may need to be shorter and simpler. For example, a unit may schedule a simple, 30-minute surprise evaluation each week that does not involve live-fire or external support. Then, once per month, the unit will conduct a more established evaluation that might last several hours or even all day, incorporating live fire and other training resources. Finally, once per quarter, the unit may conduct an extended, realistic simulation/evaluation. This is just an example of a potential evaluation schedule.

The example above shows how a unit with limited time and resources might structure an evaluation schedule. Ideally, a unit should conduct evaluations even more frequently. The best way to accomplish this is to incorporate evaluations into daily training evolutions. Units that achieve very high levels of performance frequently integrate evaluations into almost every training activity. There is always a "standard" or "par-time" for each activity and unit members who fail to meet established standards can face adverse action.

The only way for a unit to identify the ideal evaluation schedule is to experiment with different options and compare the results. Over time, the unit will discover a schedule that is the best fit for mission requirements and administrative constraints. The evaluation schedule may be adjusted over time to keep pace with changes in the situation.

STEP 6: Execute Evaluations and Record Results

Combat performance evaluation results are difficult to measure and quantify. Some aspects of an evaluation can be recorded and scored (like speed of movement, shooting accuracy etc.) but others will require more detailed evaluation. The best way to accomplish this is to film each combat performance evaluation and then review the video afterwards as a unit, much like how a sports team analyzes film from the last game. There are no fixed formulas for evaluating or scoring combat performance evaluations so it is best to use your common sense, measuring what can be measured and using analytical thinking to examine the rest.

FINAL POINTS

Any individual citizen or organization can benefit from a combat performance evaluation. The key is to analyze what your real-life combat requirements might be and design your tests accordingly. The examples above are only a few options for creating a combat performance evaluation. By being creative and sharing ideas with your peers, you should have no probelm coming up with effective test options that fit your mission requirements. Ideally, combat performance evaluations should focus not only on the most likely real-world scenarios, but also on the most dangerous or "worst-case" scenarios.

If possible, you should time every event and track performance over an extended period. Most importantly, it is critical that every test be a surprise. If your people know when the test is coming and know what will be on it, you will be unable to assess their true level of readiness.

SECTION 1

EXERCISE & TRAINING TECHNIQUES

EXERCISE & TRAINING TECHNIQUES
Mobility Training

Mobility is essential for all combat operations and should form a critical part of any combat fitness program. The type and focus of mobility training may vary depending on mission requirements. Mobility training may include running, climbing, obstacle negotiation, swimming, hiking (rucking), plyometrics, agility and speed training. Rather than looking at each of these types of exercises in isolation, it is more useful to combine them all under the heading of "mobility" and think about how the various exercises might help you move faster, farther and more efficiently in a real combat situation.

In real combat, you might have to move while carrying heavy loads or over rough terrain. Therefore, if you only conduct mobility training on a flat surface in shorts and a tee-shirt, you may not be prepared for the demands of real combat. However, moving in full gear or moving over difficult terrain can be very taxing on the body and increase your chances of injury. It is best to balance higher-impact mobility training with lower-impact mobility training. One key point to remember is that it is generally not a good idea to jog long distances carrying a rucksack or gear. In most combat situations when you are moving under a load, you will be either walking long distances or sprinting short distances. Therefore, jogging under a load is not very realistic and puts a great deal of unnecessary stress on the legs and joints.

The best balance usually involves conducting most of your mobility training without a combat load on a flat surface or evenly sloped hills. This will help build speed and strength while minimizing the chances of injury. Then, once or twice per week you can conduct mobility training under load or on difficult terrain. It can also be useful to practice moving at night, through dense brush, thick mud, or in other difficult conditions.

RUNNING FORM

Distance Running Form (1 of 2)

Before beginning any running workout or routine it is critical to learn the proper running form. Good form will reduce the chances of injury and build muscle memory for biomechanically correct movements. The form for distance running is similar to the form for sprinting but there are some minor differences. Below are a series of steps and guidelines for learning and maintaining the correct form for distance running.

1 STAY TALL: Stand as straight and tall as possible, keeping your back straight. Avoid hunching forward or letting your spine curve in either direction. Your chin should be slightly tucked and your shoulders should be relaxed.

2 FORWARD LEAN: Lean forward slightly so your center of gravity is in front of your feet. This will give you the sensation of "falling forward" and provide momentum to help make running easier and faster.

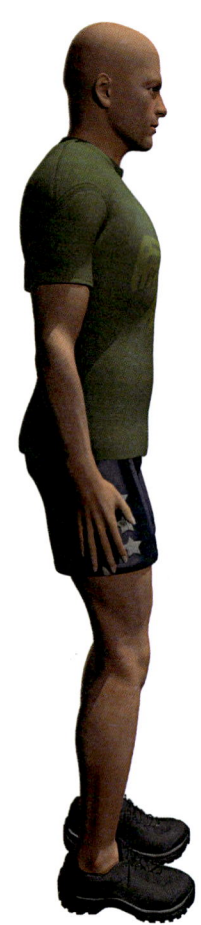
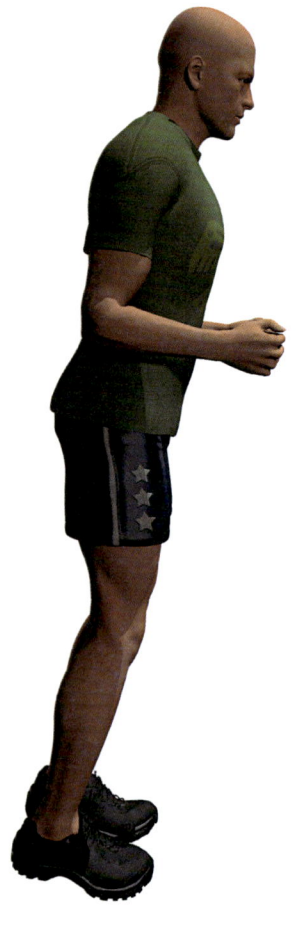

RUNNING FORM

Distance Running Form (2 of 4)

3 FOOT STRIKE: As you fall forward, you will need to "catch yourself" with one of your feet to keep from falling on your face. Catching yourself over and over as you fall forward is essentially what running is. Striking the ground with the mid-foot generally improves speed and reduces impact on the joints.

4 SHOCK ABSORPTION: Your foot should strike the ground in a gentle and coordinated manner. If your feet are smacking the ground and making a lot of noise it means you are not absorbing shock properly.

RUNNING FORM

Distance Running Form (3 of 4)

5 **PUSH OFF:** This is the portion of the running movement that actually propels you forward. Pushing off through your toe and getting the maximum extension out of your leg will help you run more efficiently.

6 **LEG CYCLE:** After pushing off, your leg must cycle around to strike the ground again. Your foot should rise up towards your buttocks as your knee drives forward. How high the leg cycles through and how high the knee comes up depends on how fast you are running.

RUNNING FORM

Distance Running Form (4 of 4)

7 ARM MOVEMENT: Keep the shoulders relaxed and the elbows close to the body. The hands should remain relaxed as well, not clenched in fists or stiff like a knife hand. The arms should move forward and back in the direction of travel instead of coming across the body.

8 BREATHING: Breathing should remain as relaxed and controlled as possible. If the chest starts heaving it can cause you to arch your back, tense your shoulders and lose your form.

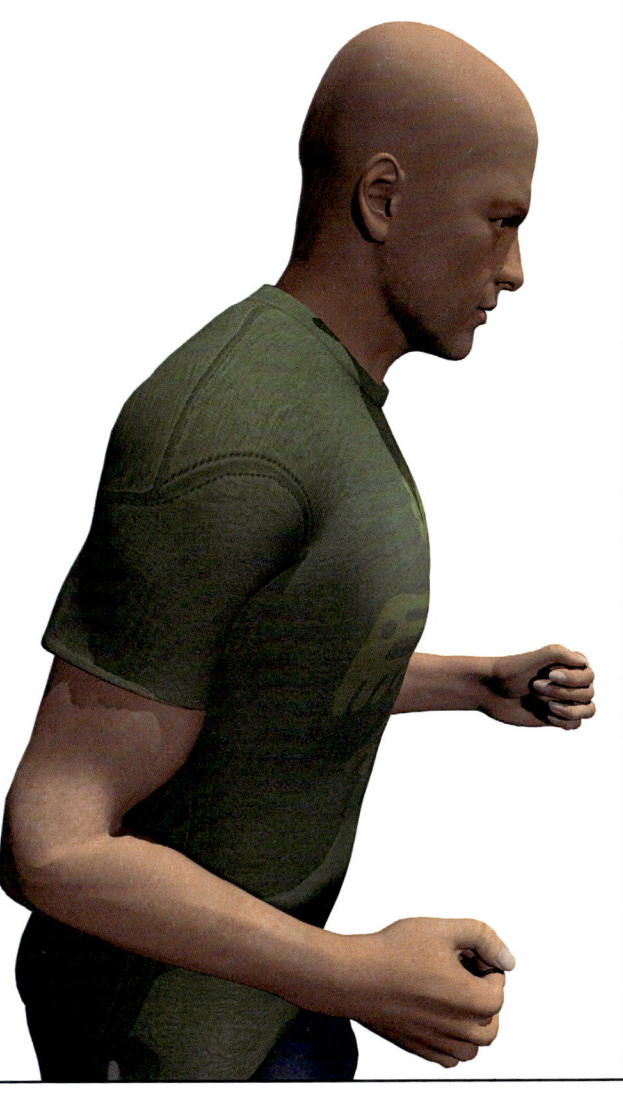

RUNNING FORM

Sprinting Form (1 of 4)

Form is particularly important for sprinting since incorrect form can increase your chances of injury or loss of balance. The running form for sprinting differs from the form for distance running in several ways as explained in the guidelines below.

1 **STAY TALL:** Stand as straight and tall as possible, keeping your back straight. Avoid hunching forward or letting your spine curve in either direction. Your chin should be slightly tucked and your shoulders should be relaxed.

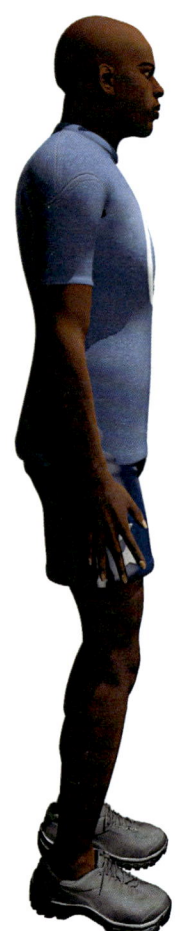

2 **FORWARD LEAN:** Lean forward so your center of gravity is in front of your feet. This will give you the sensation of "falling forward" and provide momentum to help you run faster. The forward lean for sprinting is much more aggressive than in distance running.

RUNNING FORM

Sprinting Form (2 of 4)

3 **FOOT STRIKE:** As you fall forward, you will need to "catch yourself" with one of your feet to keep from falling on your face. Catching yourself over and over as you fall forward is essentially what running is. For sprinting, you should strike the ground with your toe.

4 **PUSH OFF:** The push off for spiriting should be much more powerful and aggressive than for distance running. It is critical to fire the leg downward and back, getting the full extension out of the leg and pushing off the toe.

RUNNING FORM

Sprinting Form (3 of 4)

5 LEG CYCLE: After pushing off, your leg must cycle around to strike the ground again. Your foot should snap back towards your buttocks as your knee drives forward. It is critical to cycle the leg through high, with your cycling foot passing through at the same level or higher than the opposite knee.

6 KNEE DRIVE: The knee should come up higher as well. Driving the knee forward is essentially a "wind up" for the next foot strike. As the knee is driving up and forward, the opposite leg is driving into the ground and pushing off.

RUNNING FORM

Sprinting Form (4 of 4)

7 ARM MOVEMENT: Keep your elbows close to the body and your hands and shoulders relaxed. The arms should move forward and back in the direction of travel instead of coming across the body. The hands should travel from a point even with the shoulder to a point even with the hip bone.

8 ELBOW DRIVE: A critical component of the arm movement is driving your elbows back and keeping your elbows from popping out in a chicken wing motion. Driving the elbows back and cycling the arms as fast as possible will greatly increase running speed.

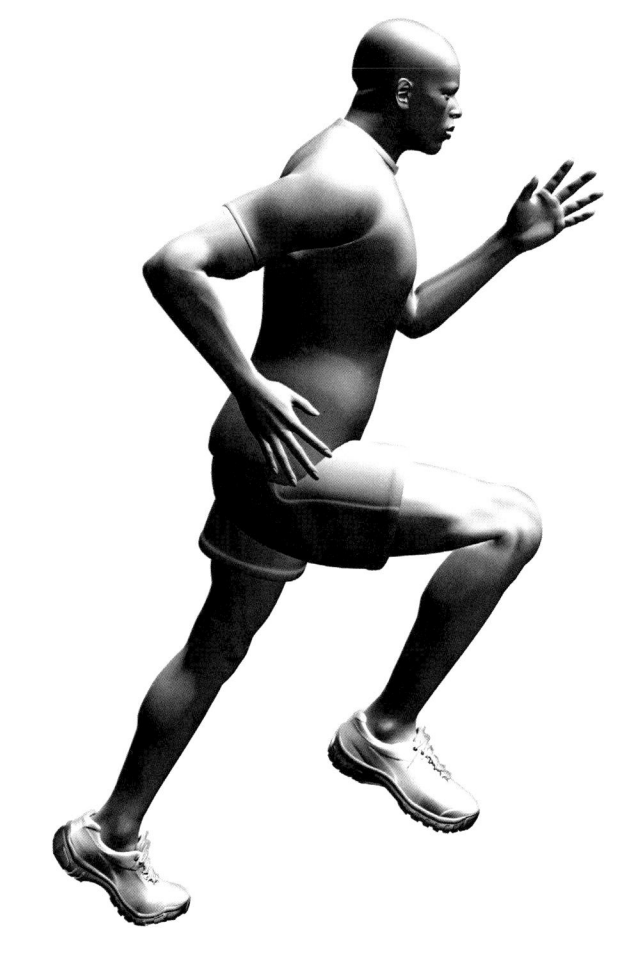
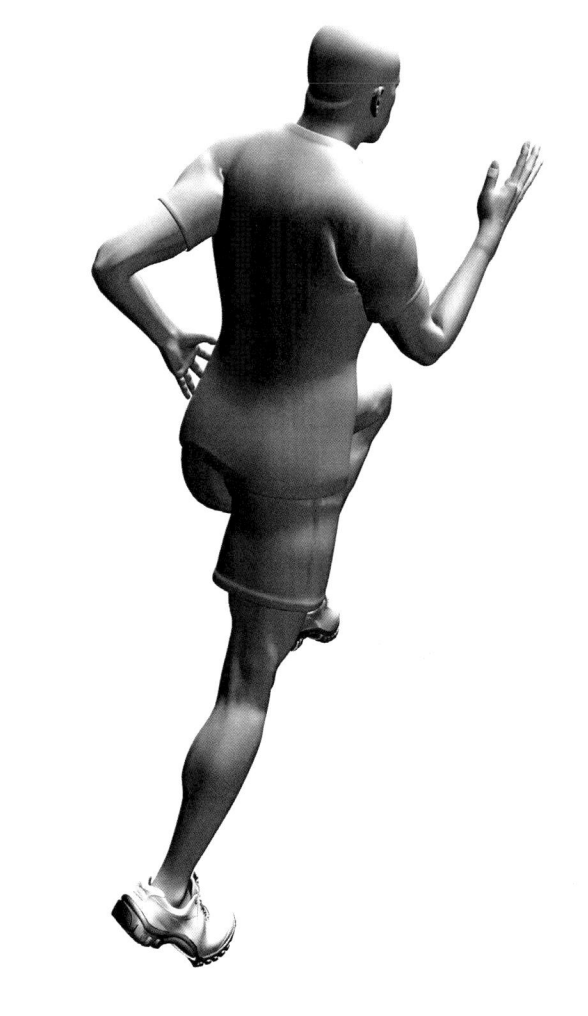

RUNNING DRILLS

Tall and Fall (1 of 2)

Running drills are a great way to improve running form and build strength, flexibility and coordination in the areas critical for running. The tall and fall drill helps develop the correct posture and forward lean required for efficient running. The tall and fall drill can also be used to begin many of the other running and agility drills.

1 **STARTING POSITION:** Begin by standing upright with correct posture with your shoulders relaxed, and your chin tucked slightly. Try to stand as tall as possible, reaching for the sky with the top of your head.

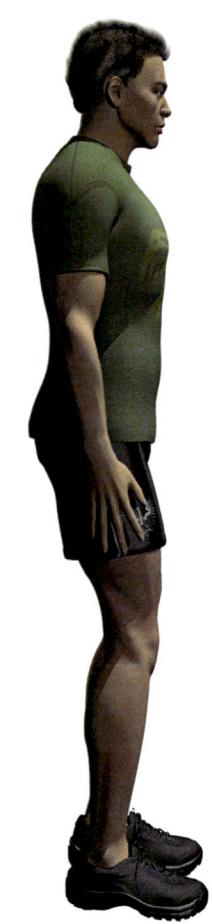

2 **FORWARD LEAN:** Lean forward so your center of gravity is in front of your feet. This will give you the sensation of "falling forward" and provide momentum to help you run faster. The forward lean for sprinting is much more aggressive than in distance running.

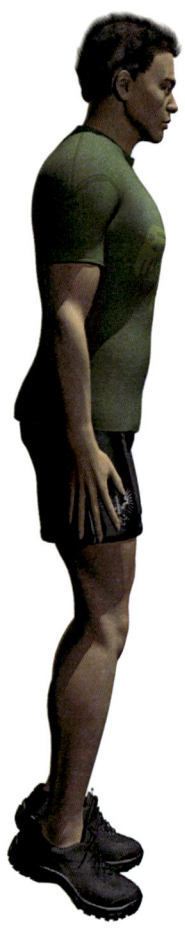

RUNNING DRILLS

Tall and Fall (2 of 2)

3 FALL FORWARD: Let yourself fall forward slowly while keeping your feet in place and maintaining a straight, tall posture.

4 RUN THROUGH: At a certain point, you will have to step forward and catch yourself so you do not fall on your face. Once you step forward break into a relaxed, natural run for about 10 yards.

RUNNING DRILLS

High Knees (1 of 2)

The high knees drill is particularly helpful for improving speed and sprinting ability. The high knees drill builds strength in the hip flexors and flexibility in the hips and hamstrings. It helps improve explosive speed and improves running form and posture.

1 **STARTING POSITION:** Begin the high knees drill with the tall and fall drill.

2 **DRIVE THROUGH THE TOE:** To raise the knee properly, you must drive the opposite toe into the ground. When driving through the toe, your body should form a straight line from the top of your head to your toe. Avoid bending over or letting your waist sag forward.

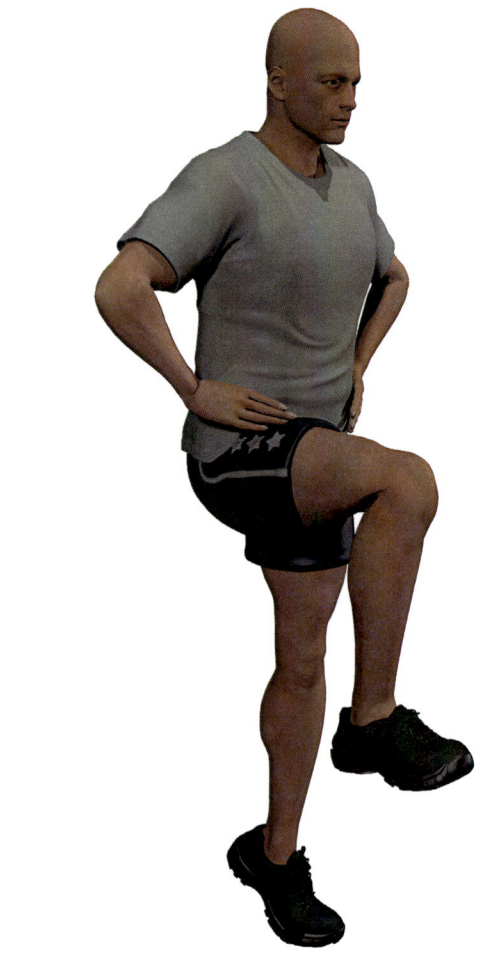

RUNNING DRILLS

High Knees (2 of 2)

3 **RAISE THE KNEE UP:** Driving downward through the toe with as much force as possible will naturally help the knee raise up. Lift the knee until your upper leg is parallel to the ground. Avoid letting the hips sink forward or back. Maintain good posture and a forward lean.

4 **ARM MOVEMENT:** You can either conduct the drill with your hands on your hips or you can pump your arms in a running motion. If you choose to pump your arms, proper arm movement is critical to correct performance of the drill.

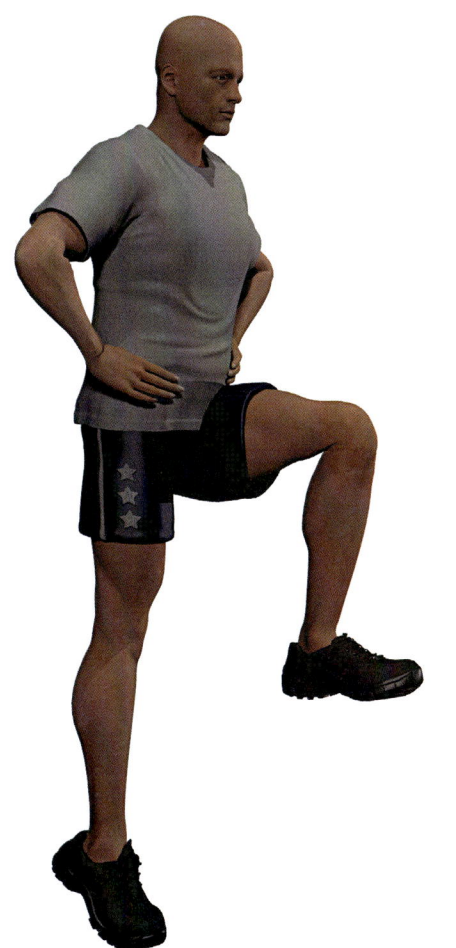
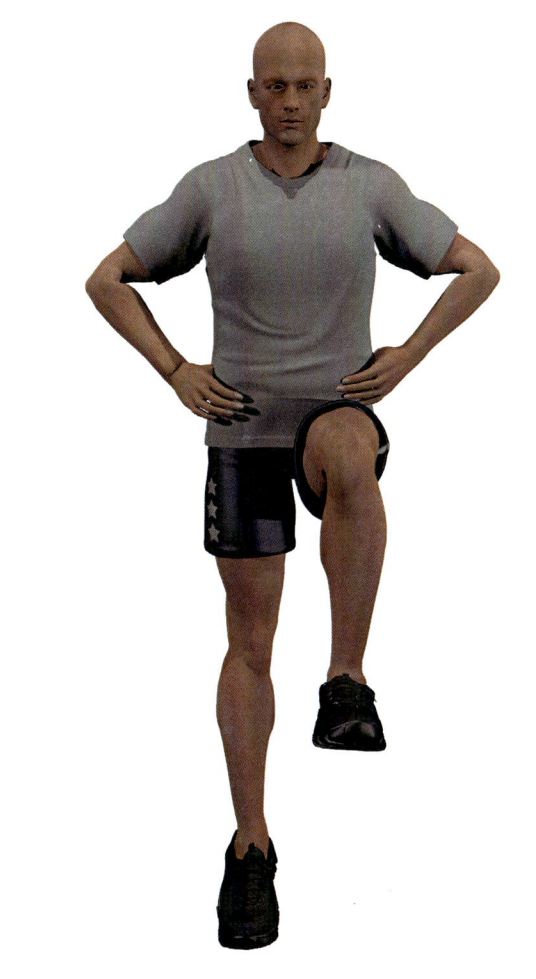

RUNNING DRILLS

Butt Kicks (1 of 2)

The butt-kick drill is particularly helpful for improving speed and sprinting ability. The butt-kick drill builds strength in the hamstrings, flexibility in the quadriceps and hip flexors. It will help improve your running form and posture.

1 **STARTING POSITION:** Begin the butt-kicks drill with the tall and fall drill.

2 **SNAP THE FOOT BACK:** Let your feet snap backwards and up towards your buttocks as you run. You do not have to actually "kick" your buttocks but you should try to bring your heel as close to the buttocks as possible.

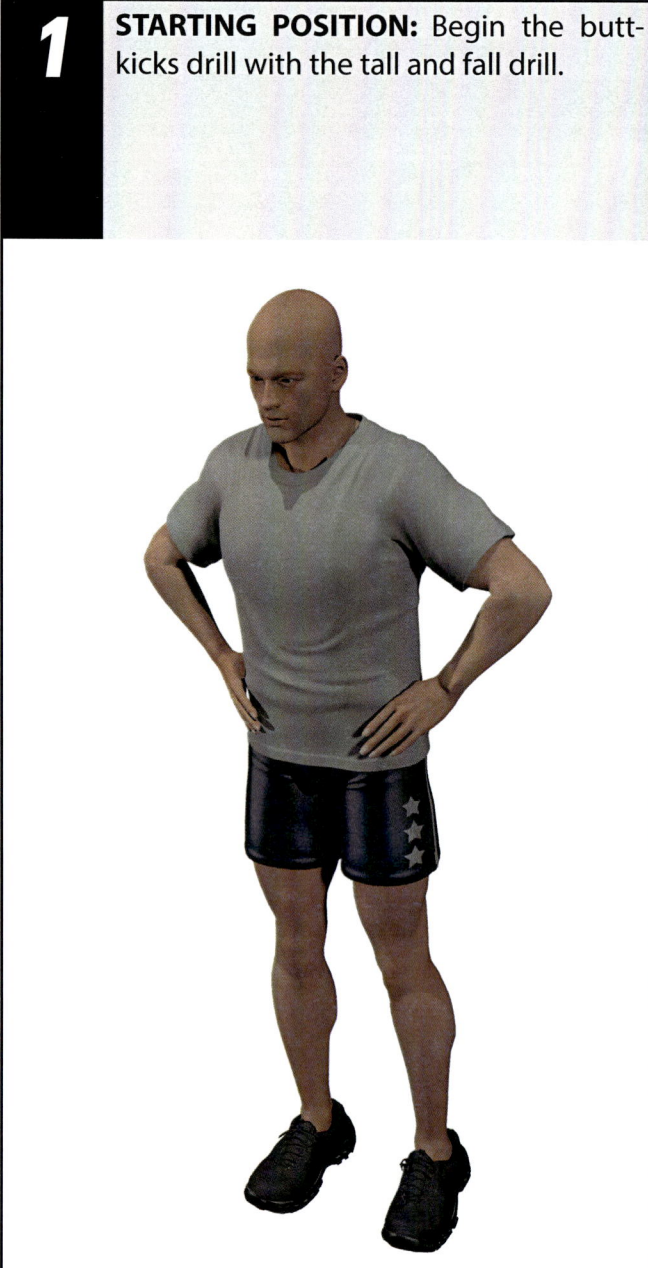

RUNNING DRILLS

Butt Kicks (2 of 2)

3 **ARM POSITION:** It can be difficult to pump your arms when conducting this drill so it is often best to keep the hands on the hips.

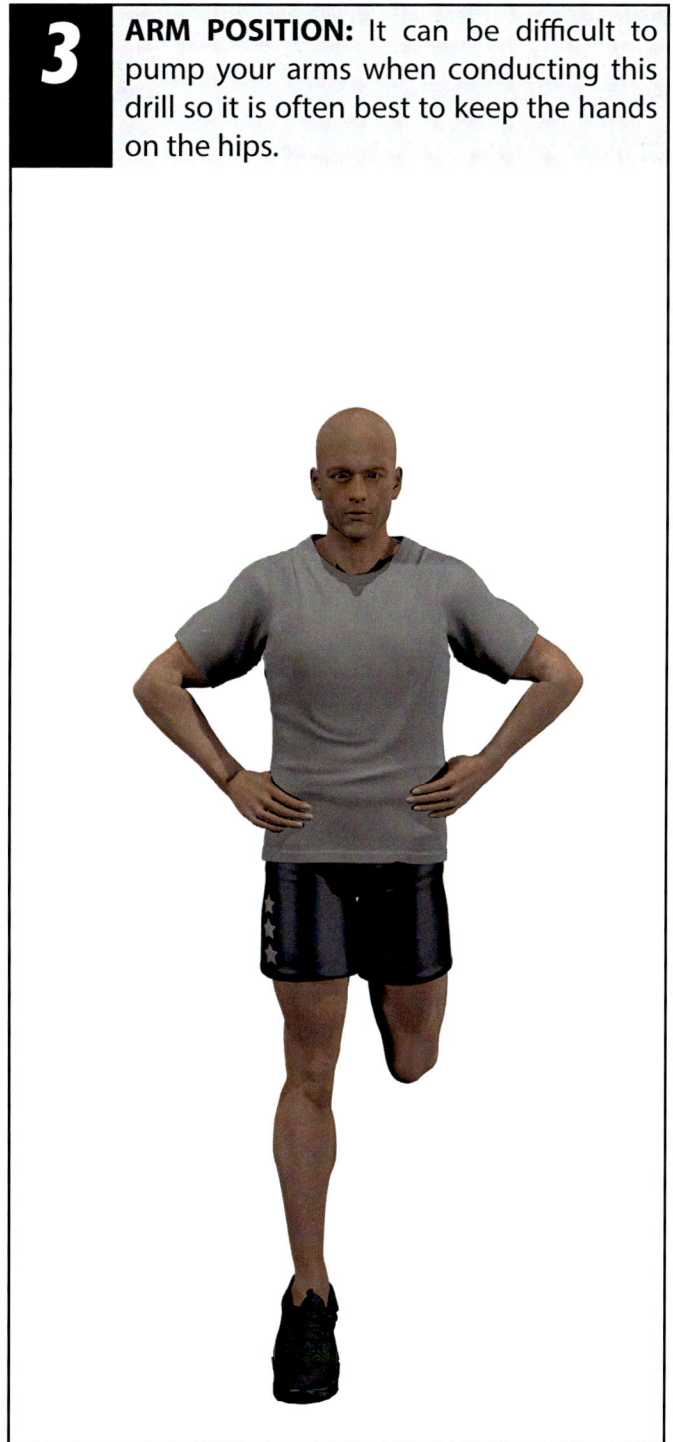

RUNNING DRILLS

Form Skips (1 of 2)

The high knees drill is particularly helpful for improving speed and sprinting ability. The high knees drill builds strength in the hip flexors, helps improve explosive speed and improves running form and posture.

1 STARTING POSITION: Begin the form skips with the tall and fall drill.

2 PUSH OFF THE GROUND: Push through the ground and drive your knee up just as in the high knees drill.

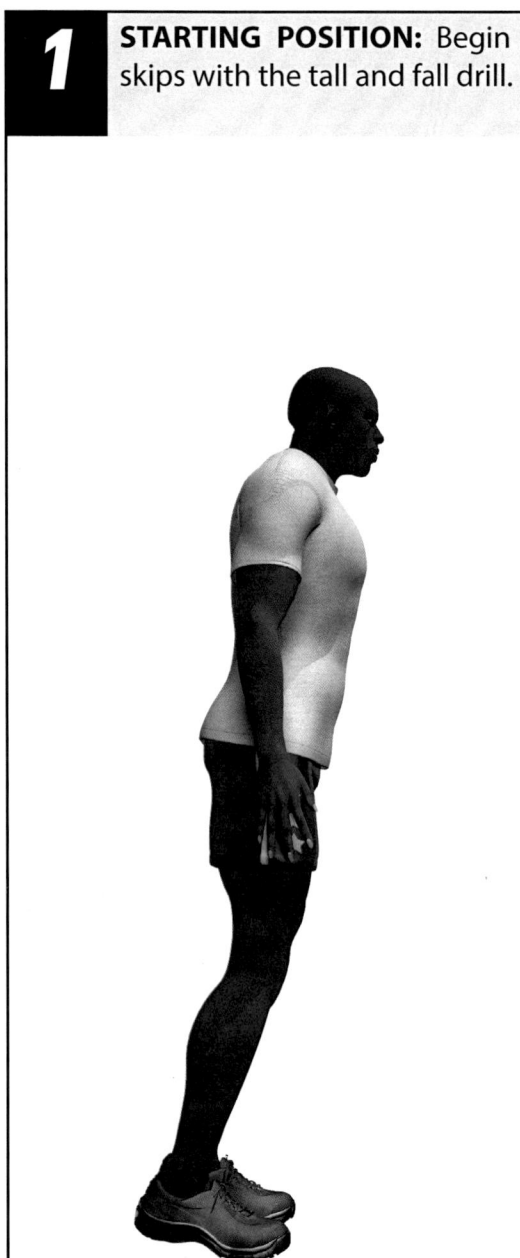

RUNNING DRILLS

Form Skips (2 of 2)

3 **SKIP FORWARD:** As you push off, let your foot come off the ground in a small forward hop, as your other foot comes back to the ground to repeat the process on the other side.

4 **ARM POSITION:** When conducting the drill, it is best to pump the arms in a slow, deliberate manner, focusing on proper form.

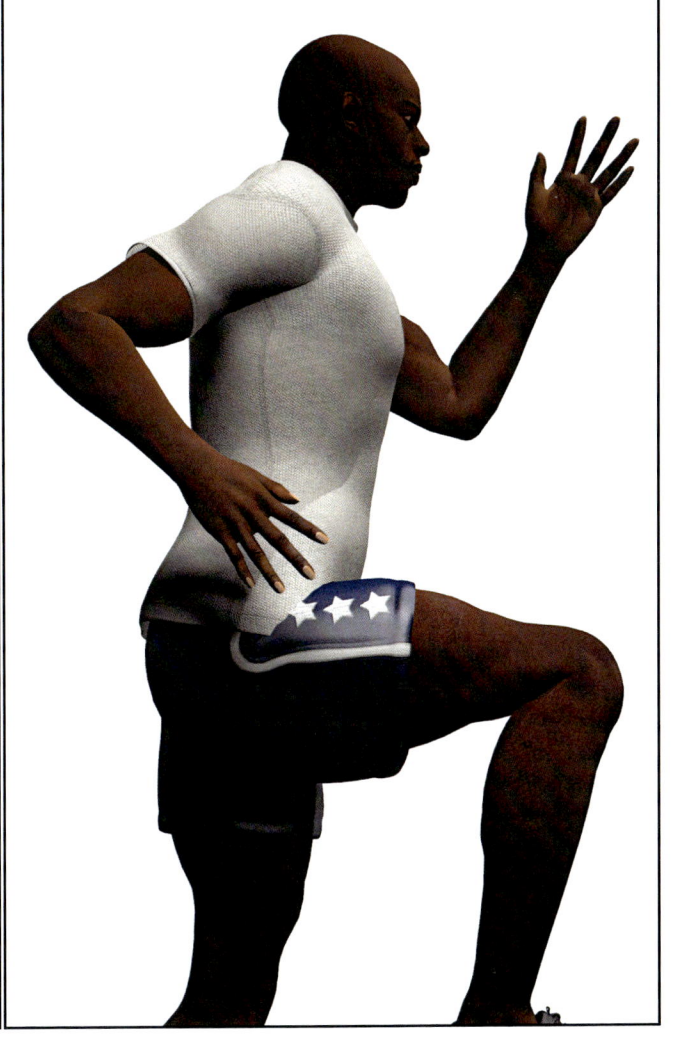

RUNNING WORKOUTS

Types of Running Workouts

There are several different types of running workouts. You should focus on workouts that build physical attributes relevant to your mission set. If your mission requirements demand strength and power, you may focus more on sprinting than long distance running. If your mission requirements demand endurance for long-range movement, distance running may prove more appropriate. Regardless of the area of focus, some level of running ability is critical for most combat disciplines and you should incorporate one or more of the following types of workouts into your running routine.

DISTANCE RUNS: Distance running helps build the cardiovascular endurance and muscle endurance necessary for traveling long distances by foot. Distance running also strengthens bones, joints, ligaments and calluses, allowing you to exert yourself for longer periods of time without risking injury. For this reason, distance running is a good starting point for building a running routine since it prepares your body to absorb the punishment caused by running workouts. When you can run 10 miles comfortably, your cardiovascular system, muscles, joints and feet can hold up against sustained exertion in a more combat-focused training program. Distance running generally involves running 5-miles or more with the goal of maximizing distance rather than maximizing speed. Distance running will be more useful to you if your mission set demands long-range movement and prolonged exertion. It is also important to note that if you expect to be operating with heavy gear or equipment, cross-country backpacking (rucking) might be a better choice for your needs. You may get very good at moving long distances without weight, but find that your capability drops dramatically when moving with gear or a rucksack.

TEMPO RUNS: Tempo runs still build cardiovascular and muscular endurance, but they are focused more on speed than distance. Tempo runs are usually between 2 and 5 miles. The objective is to push yourself to complete the run in a specific target time (tempo) or to complete the run as fast as possible, attempting to beat your best time or "personal record" (PR). Tempo runs are a good choice if you are looking for a balanced running workout. They will improve both your endurance and speed without putting excessive strain on your joints.

ENDURANCE INTERVALS: Endurance intervals call for running a shorter distance (often between 200m and 800m) multiple times with minimal rest (usually 1-2 minutes) in-between. For example, an endurance interval workout might call for running a total of 4 x 800m sprints in under 2:30 with 2-minutes rest between each one. In order for endurance intervals to be effective, you should never feel fully recovered after the rest period. The goal is to learn to push yourself when you are winded and fatigued. Endurance intervals can sometimes allow you to push yourself harder than you can on a regular tempo or distance run. By breaking the run into parts, it is easier to exert maximum effort in each part.

RUNNING WORKOUTS

Types of Running Workouts (cont)

SPEED INTERVALS: Speed intervals are similar to sprints but they typically involve running longer distances (200m to 1 mile). When running speed intervals, you will take a much longer rest period or in some cases, you will take as much rest as you need. For example, a speed interval workout might call for running a total of 4x400m sprints at full speed with full recovery in between each one. Speed intervals help you build your running speed and leg strength. The goal is less to tax the cardiovascular system, but more to push the muscles to their limits.

SPRINTS: Sprints are designed to build your speed and develop the fast-twitch muscle fibers in your legs. You can only build speed when you are pushing your own personal speed barrier. If your fastest 200m sprint is 22 seconds, as long as you are running your sprints in 23 or 24 seconds you are training your speed because you are operating at the threshold of your ability to move your legs and arms quickly. However, if because of fatigue you start dropping down to 27 or 28 seconds, you are no longer building speed, you are building strength and endurance. Therefore, sprints involve pushing yourself to move as fast as possible before you are fatigued. For this reason, sprint training usually involves shorter distances below 200m. It is often best to take as much recovery time as possible between each sprint.

HILL INTERVALS/SPRINTS: You can conduct endurance intervals, speed intervals or sprints up a hill in order to increase the difficulty and intensity of the workout. Hill training is one of the most effective running workouts. When you are used to running hills, you will find it much easier to run on flat ground and your running speed and endurance will increase more rapidly. If you do not have access to a hill, running stairs can be equally effective. Also, if you operate primarily in an urban environment, stairs might be a better fit for your mission requirements.

RECOVERY RUNS: Recovery runs are not designed to push the limits in either speed or distance. Rather, they are relaxed runs for a planned time interval, designed to stimulate blood flow and clear lactic acid buildup from the muscles. Recovery runs will also contribute to endurance and leg strength over time. Recovery runs are a good option for maintaining your running ability when you are fatigued or tired from other workouts.

SPEED WALKING: If your operational requirements might include long-distance marches carrying a load, speed walking is an effective, low-impact way to increase marching speed. Sometimes fast runners have difficulty moving quickly carrying a pack or ruck because they are not used to walking fast and taking big steps. Speed walking can help solve this problem.

RUNNING WORKOUTS

Running Routines

It is generally not a good idea to run every day, since doing so puts unnecessary strain on the joints and can cause injury. Lack of recovery time can also slow the rate of overall progress. Instead, it is best to run at most every-other-day and to incorporate a variety of different running workouts into your routine. As already mentioned, you should focus on workouts that build specific capabilities for your mission requirements. Below are some examples of running routines, based on this model.

SPEED FOCUSED ROUTINE

SUNDAY	MONDAY	TUESDAY	WEDNESDAY	THURSDAY	FRIDAY	SATURDAY
NO RUNNING	2-Mile Tempo Run	NO RUNNING	4 x 400m Speed Intervals (full recovery between each)	NO RUNNING	6 x 100m Sprints 5-Mile Distance Run	NO RUNNING

ENDURANCE FOCUSED ROUTINE

SUNDAY	MONDAY	TUESDAY	WEDNESDAY	THURSDAY	FRIDAY	SATURDAY
NO RUNNING	3-5 Mile Tempo Run	NO RUNNING	4 x 800m Endurance Intervals (3 min rest between each)	NO RUNNING	10-Mile Distance Run	NO RUNNING

HEAVY ROUTINE

SUNDAY	MONDAY	TUESDAY	WEDNESDAY	THURSDAY	FRIDAY	SATURDAY
NO RUNNING	6 x 100m Sprints 3-Mile Tempo Run	NO RUNNING	Pyramid Intervals: 200m, 400m, 600m, 800m, 1000m, 800m, 600m, 400m, 200m (2 min rest between each)	NO RUNNING	4 x 400m Speed Intervals (full recovery between each)	10-Mile Distance Run 6 x 100m Sprints

SPEED/AGILITY LADDER

Speed Ladder Drills

The speed/agility ladder is an effective, low-cost and lightweight training tool that can help build foot speed, agility and coordination. Foot speed and agility can prove particularly important for rapid change of direction in a combat engagement and maintaining footing when moving under fire or over rough terrain. To employ the ladder, lay it out on a flat surface. A hard surface like concrete or a gym floor is usually best. The goal is to move through the ladder as quickly as possible. There are many different step patterns, each one offering different benefits in terms of mobility. Below are some examples of common and effective step patterns. The numbers indicate the sequence of steps.

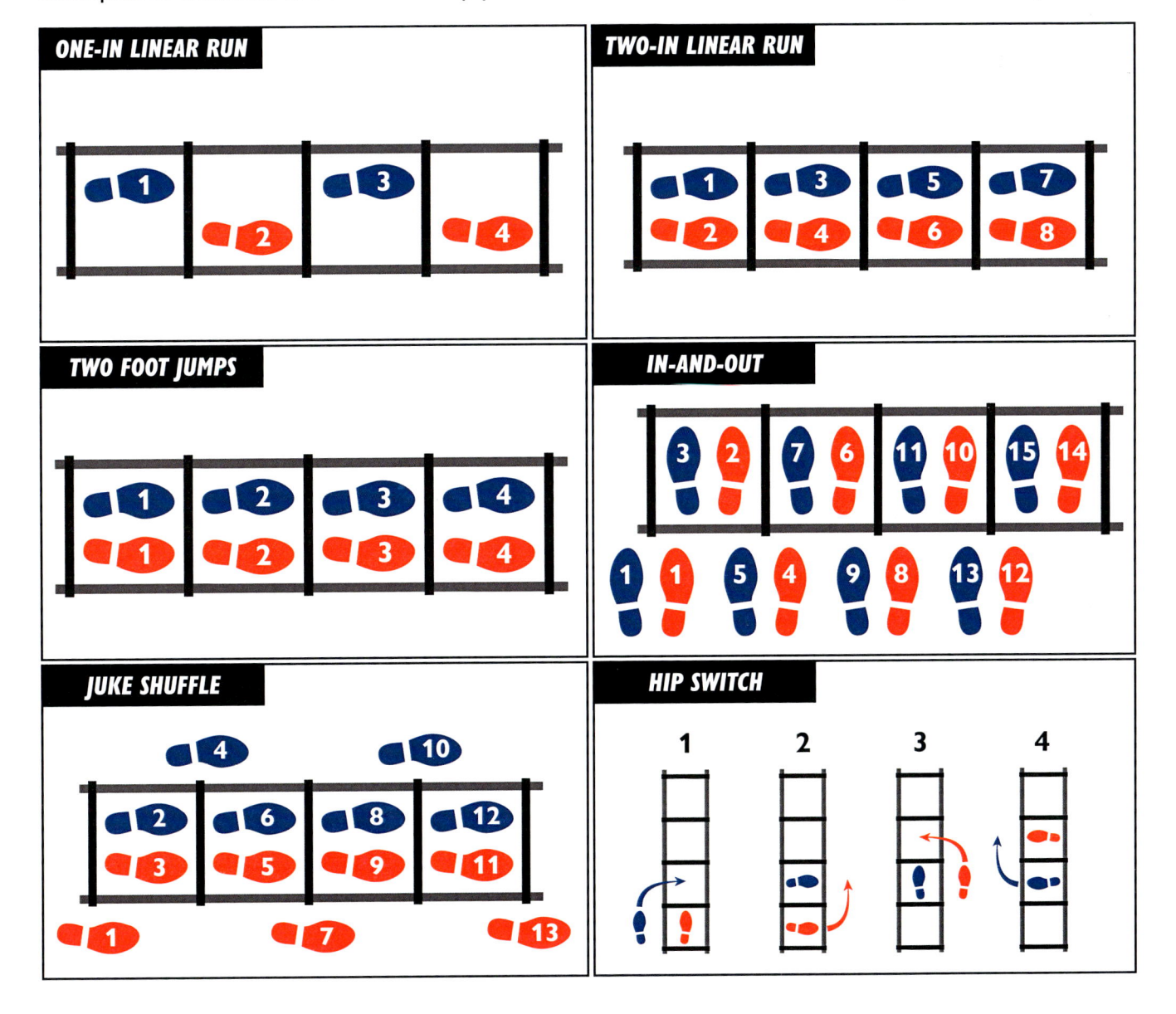

ONE-IN LINEAR RUN

TWO-IN LINEAR RUN

TWO FOOT JUMPS

IN-AND-OUT

JUKE SHUFFLE

HIP SWITCH

POWER PLYOMETRICS

Box Drop (1 of 2)

The ability to jump and land correctly can prove very useful in a combat situation. In addition, the explosive leg strength built through plyometrics can greatly improve running speed, agility and the ability to change direction quickly. The most basic plyometric drills are the box drop and box jump. It is good to master these drills before attempting more complex plyometric movements since they will help you learn the correct jumping form and landing technique. Before you attempt the box jump, you should first practice landing with the box drop drill.

1 DROP OFF: Stand at the edge of the box with your weight on your toes. Fall forward gently and let your feet drop off the edge of the box.

2 CATCH THE GROUND: While you should not "reach for the ground," let your toes extend slightly and let your relaxed legs hover below you. The goal is to gently "catch" the ground with your toes, keeping your legs as relaxed as possible.

POWER PLYOMETRICS

Box Drop (2 of 2)

3 **ABSORB THE SHOCK:** Once your toes make contact with the ground, roll on to your full feet and drop your hips down and back into a correct squat position. The goal is to land as quietly as possible.

4 **RECOVER:** Once you land and absorb the shock, stand back upright using correct squat form.

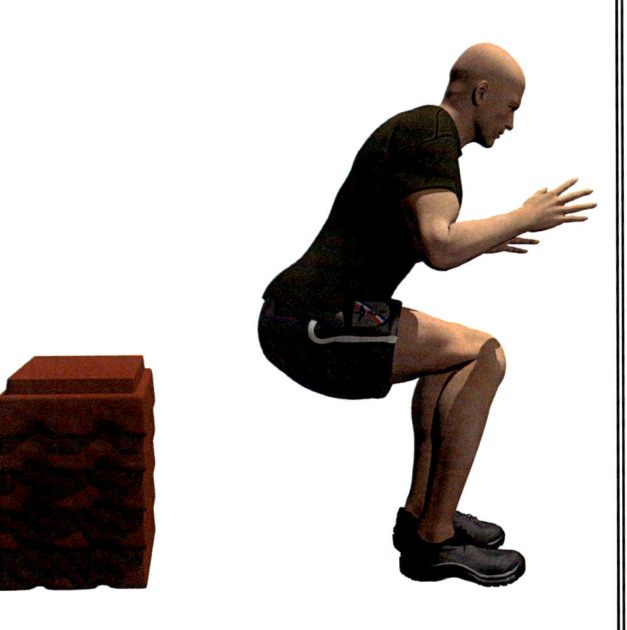

POWER PLYOMETRICS

Box Jump (1 of 2)

Once you have practiced landing and are able to land quietly, absorbing shock with your legs, you are ready to move on to the box jump. Even if you are an experienced athlete, it is important to practice landing extensively before performing a large volume of plyometric exercises, since the impact of jumping can cause strain and injury. As you get better at the box jump you can attempt to jump onto higher and higher boxes.

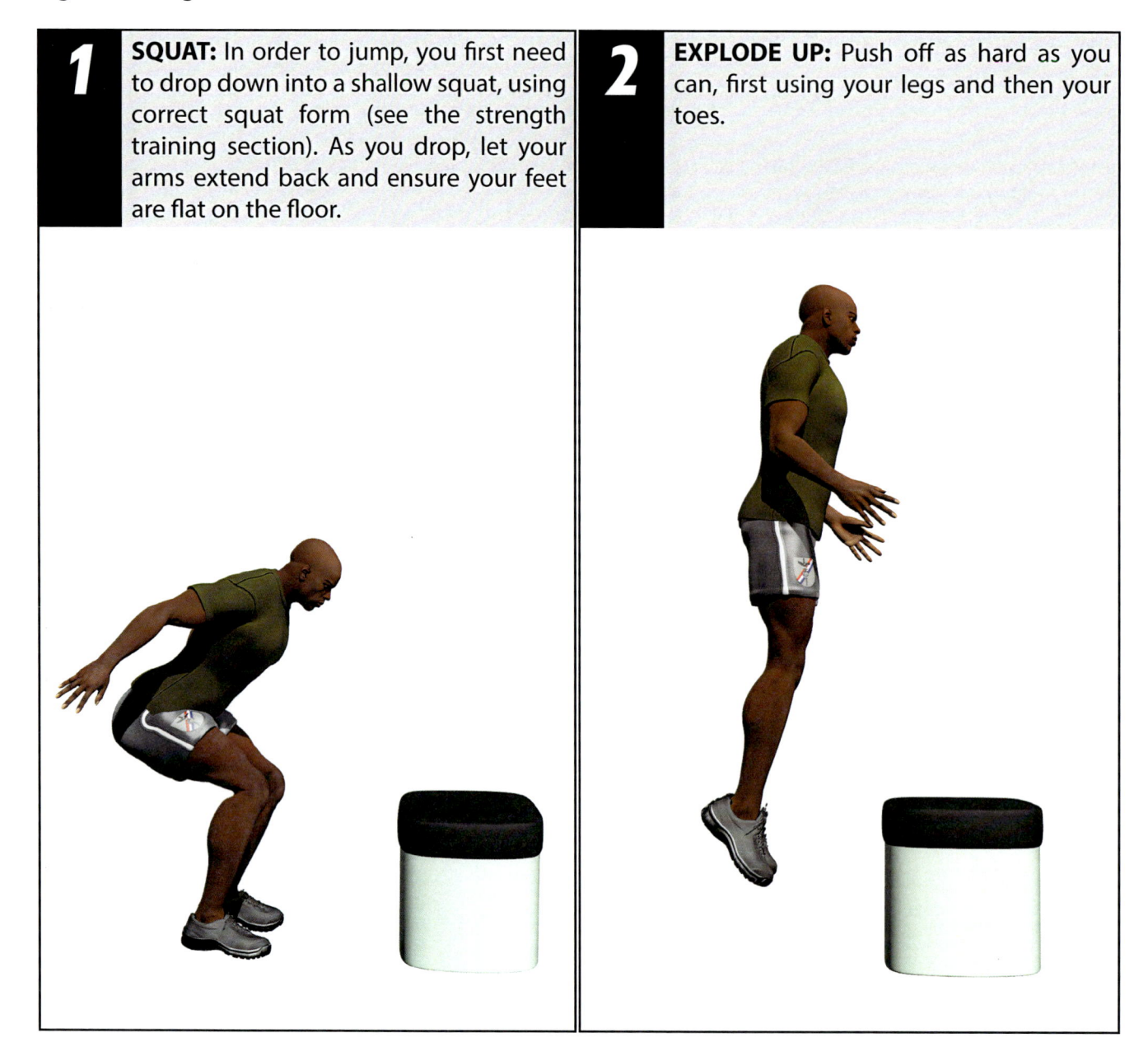

1. SQUAT: In order to jump, you first need to drop down into a shallow squat, using correct squat form (see the strength training section). As you drop, let your arms extend back and ensure your feet are flat on the floor.

2. EXPLODE UP: Push off as hard as you can, first using your legs and then your toes.

POWER PLYOMETRICS

Box Jump (2 of 2)

3 **RETRACT THE LEGS:** As you come off the ground, lift your knees and flex your toes up to prepare to land on the box. In addition, as you rise, your arms will come forward to a comfortable position in front of you.

4 **SOFT LANDING:** Land on the balls of your feet and then let your legs absorb the shock of your landing as you sink into a squat position. You should practice landing as quietly as possible. This is an indicator that you are absorbing shock properly.

POWER PLYOMETRICS

Linear Hops (1 of 2)

The form for conducting linear hops is the same as used for the box jump, except when jumping forward, the landing will require you to let your legs float forward to absorb your forward momentum. As you get better at linear hops, you can attempt to jump longer distances. You can begin by performing two-foot hops and then move on to one-foot hops. One-foot hops demand much more leg strength and are also a great way to develop balance, especially if you perform the hops along a straight line painted on the ground.

1 SQUAT: In order to jump, you first need to drop down into a shallow squat, using correct squat form (see the strength training section). As you drop, let your arms extend back and ensure your feet are flat on the floor.

2 EXPLODE UP AND FORWARD: Push off as hard as you can. As you come off the ground, lift your knees and let your arms come forward to a comfortable position in front of you.

POWER PLYOMETRICS

Linear Hops (2 of 2)

3 **PREPARE TO LAND:** As you come down, extend your toes slightly and let your feet float forward in order to absorb your forward momentum.

4 **SOFT LANDING:** Land on the balls of your feet and then let your legs absorb the shock of your landing as you sink into a squat position. You should practice landing as quietly as possible. This is an indicator that you are absorbing shock properly.

POWER PLYOMETRICS

Diagonal Hops (1 of 2)

Diagonal hops are similar to linear hops except that they help you practice the specific techniques for landing diagonally. It is also possible to practice lateral hops (straight to the left and right) using essentially the same technique but the diagonal movement is more common and functional for combat situations. It is also possible to perform one-foot diagonal hops.

1 SQUAT: In order to jump, you first need to drop down into a shallow squat, using correct squat form. As you drop, let your arms extend back and ensure your feet are flat on the floor.

2 EXPLODE UP AND DIAGONALLY: Push off as hard as you can so you travel forward at about a 45-degree angle. As you come off the ground, lift your knees and let your arms come forward to a comfortable position in front of you.

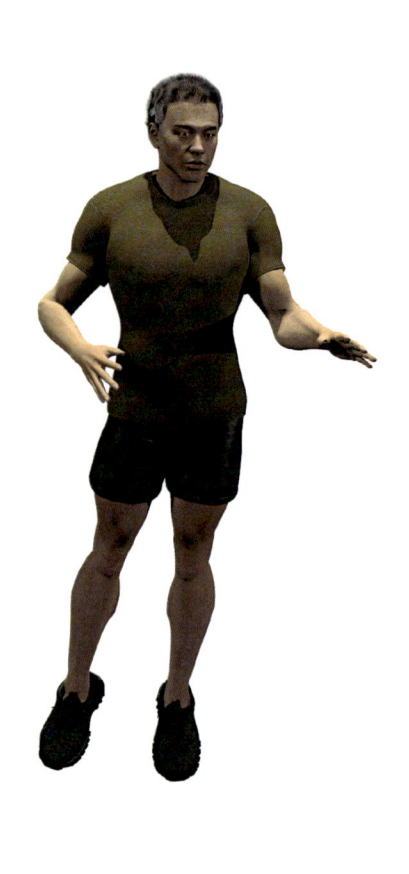

POWER PLYOMETRICS

Diagonal Hops (2 of 2)

3 **PREPARE TO LAND:** As you come down, extend your toes slightly and let your feet float forward and to the side (in the direction you are moving) in order to absorb your forward momentum.

4 **SOFT LANDING:** As you land, let the ball of your rear foot (in relation to the direction you are moving) come down first, then roll on to your front foot. For example, if you jump diagonally to the right, let your left foot land first. Let your legs absorb the shock of your landing as you sink into a squat position.

SPEED PLYOMETRICS

Six-Count

Power plyometrics help build your ability to jump higher and farther. Speed plyometrics help build foot speed, agility and the ability to change direction. One of the most effective and versatile speed plyometrics exercises is the six-count. The six-count develops leg strength, foot speed and hip rotation. When conducting speed plyometrics it is best to use a smaller box, approximately 12 inches high. Conduct the exercise as quickly as possible and conduct more repetitions to increase difficulty.

1) FORWARD BOX JUMP: Start facing the box and jump forward onto it, using correct form.

2) DROP OFF: Continue moving forward, dropping off the edge of the box and landing with correct form.

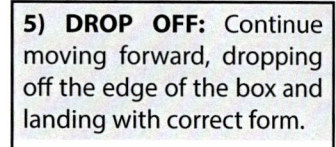

3) 180-DEGREE SPIN: Jump and spin 180-degrees so you are facing the box once again.

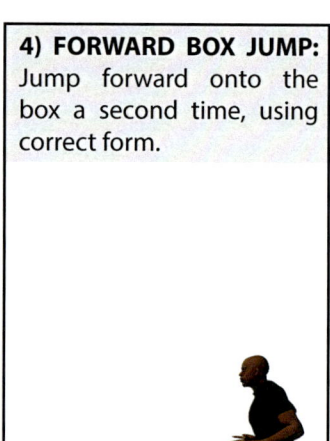

4) FORWARD BOX JUMP: Jump forward onto the box a second time, using correct form.

5) DROP OFF: Continue moving forward, dropping off the edge of the box and landing with correct form.

6) 180-DEGREE SPIN: Jump and spin 180-degrees so you are facing the box once again.

7) REPEAT: Once you have completed the six-count, you are back in position to repeat the movement.

SPEED PLYOMETRICS

Lateral Box Hops

Lateral box hops are similar to the six-count except they focus primarily on lateral movement and change of direction. When conducting speed plyometrics it is best to use a smaller box, approximately 12 inches high. Conduct the exercise as quickly as possible. Conduct more repetitions to increase difficulty and build cardiovascular endurance.

1) LATERAL BOX JUMP: Start with the box to your side and jump laterally onto it, using correct form.

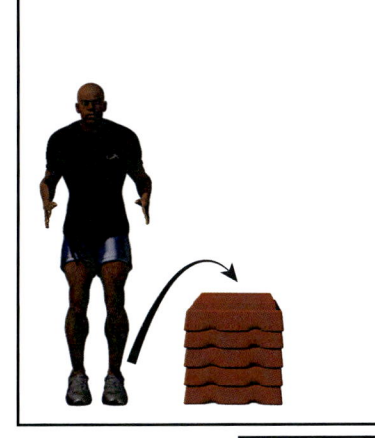

2) DROP OFF: Continue moving laterally, dropping off the edge of the box and landing with correct form.

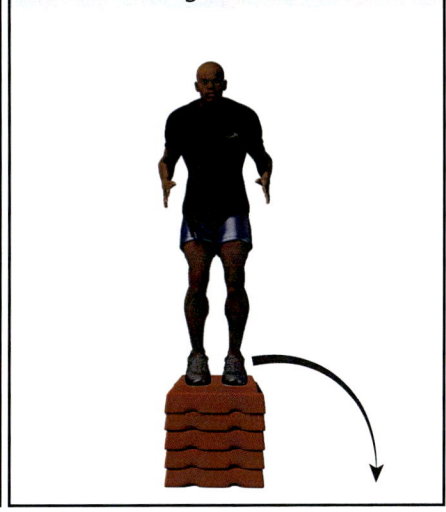

3) LATERAL BOX JUMP: Jump laterally in the opposite direction onto the box using correct form.

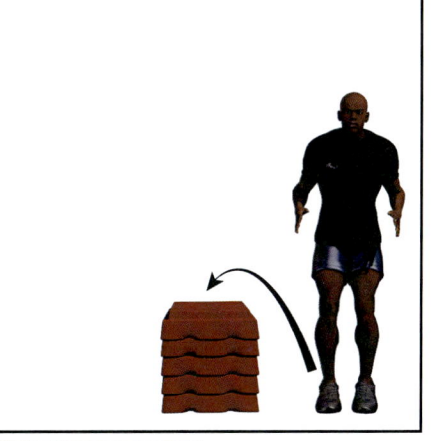

4) DROP OFF: Continue moving laterally, dropping off the edge of the box and landing back in the starting position.

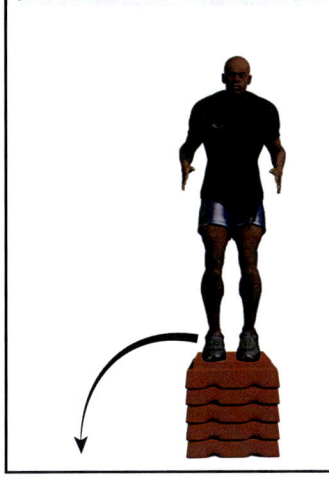

5) REPEAT: Once you have completed the four counts of the exercise, you are back in position to repeat the movement.

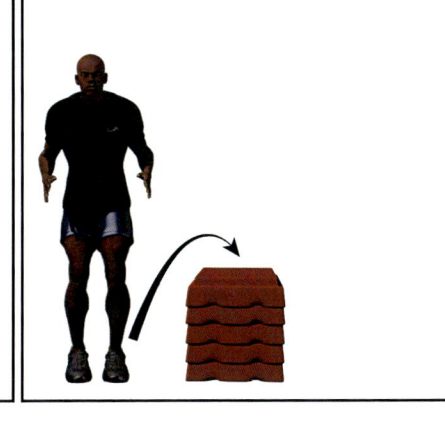

CROSS-COUNTRY MOVEMENT AND RUCKING

General Guidance

There are several different types of running workouts. You should focus on workouts that build physical cross-country movement with a rucksack (backpack) is particularly important if your mission requirements include wearing or carrying heavy equipment. If all you do is distance running, you will develop very good cardiovascular endurance and the ability to run long distances. However, once you add a combat load to the equation, your capability may drop dramatically. This is because long distance running with no weight does not build the type of strength required to move under weight. Therefore, depending on your mission set, it may be important to incorporate cross-country rucking into your routine. The following points will help you develop an effective rucking routine while minimizing your chances of injury.

- While rucking is a very effective workout, it is also very taxing on the body. Therefore, it is critical to start with a relatively easy ruck (at least a 35 lb pack for 3-5 miles) and slowly build up the weight, distance and difficulty over time. If you start off carrying too much weight or moving too far, your chances of injury will be very high.

- Rucking is also very taxing on the feet and part of the goal of rucking is to toughen your feet so they can handle long distance movements in the field. The best way to toughen your feet and build calluses is to increase weight and distance over time. If you develop severe blisters and lose skin on your feet, it will toughen your feet eventually. However, in the meantime, if your feet are raw it may take away from your other workouts and slow your progress.

- Wearing the correct boots and socks is an important part of reducing the damage to your feet. Your boots should be well-fitting and broken in prior to long distance movements. Socks should be clean and dry. It is generally best to wear hiking socks that are designed to keep the feet dry and avoid abrasion. When moving very long distances, you may want to occasionally stop to change socks and apply foot powder. Also, sock changes and foot care may be in order after moving through water.

- Even when you are well conditioned for rucking, it is still preferable not to ruck more than once per week. Rucking taxes the body no matter how conditioned you are. Also, rucking less frequently will allow you to push yourself harder in terms of weight and distance. If you supplement your rucking with strength training, interval runs and hill runs, you can greatly improve your rucking ability without needing to ruck too often.

CROSS-COUNTRY MOVEMENT AND RUCKING

General Guidance (cont)

- Your pack should be well fitting and well balanced. Generally, it is best to use a civilian pack, since they have thicker shoulder and waist straps that are designed to distribute weight more effectively. Whatever pack you use, it is best to keep the weight as close to your upper back/shoulders as possible. When rucking for fitness, as opposed to a field exercise, you have the luxury of packing your ruck with a combination of pillows and sandbags (synthetic fitness sandbags are best) to distribute the weight perfectly. Fill the ruck with pillows and place the sandbag (s) as close to the upper back as possible. Then use more pillows to fix the sandbags in place.

- When wearing the pack, it is important to distribute the weight between your shoulders and waist. First, cinch the shoulder straps down as tightly as possible to get the pack high on your back. Then, attach the waist strap so it rests above your hip bones. Tighten it so it is snug but not cutting off circulation. Once the waist strap is attached, loosen the shoulder straps and feel the weight shift to your waist. Loosen and tighten the shoulder straps until it feels like the weight is evenly balanced between the waist and shoulders.

- It is generally best to ruck cross-country over rough terrain. Rucking on a paved, flat surface can be harder on the joints. Also, since it is preferable not to ruck too often, you will want to get as much as possible out of each ruck workout. Rucking over hills, cross-country is a much better workout than simply walking on the road and is more worthwhile.

- You do not need a huge space or long course to develop your cross-country rucking ability. If you have access to only one, small hill, you can have a perfectly good workout simply going up and down the hill over and over.

- It is generally best not to run with a rucksack. Running with a rucksack greatly increases the strain on the body and the chances of injury. To increase the difficulty of a ruck workout, it is better to increase weight or distance than it is to run.

- When conducting long movements, it is critical to hydrate before, during and after activity. This is especially the case in hot weather. Adding oral rehydration salts to your water can enhance your performance and reduce the risk of dehydration.

OBSTACLE COURSE TRAINING

General Guidance

Obstacle courses are one of the most effective workouts for the combat athlete. Obstacle courses simultaneously build endurance, speed, balance, coordination, upper body and lower body strength. In addition, obstacle courses teach you to quickly and safely negotiate obstacles that might be similar to obstacles you encounter in real operations. The following points will help you develop an effective obstacle course training program.

- The best training obstacles are generally the simple ones like walls of different heights, ropes, ladders, balance beams, drain pipes etc. There are some obstacles that are more complicated and require strange contortions of the body. These may still prove useful but they are not as useful as the more realistic obstacles.

- If you do not have access to a real obstacle course, it is often easy to find obstacles in the environment. You can pick running or rucking routes that take you past these obstacles so you can incorporate them into your training routine. Some good obstacles include: walls of various heights, fallen trees, ladders, large boulders and fences. Children's playgrounds can also have interesting obstacles and are generally unoccupied at night or early morning.

- It is best to begin by running through the obstacle course without any gear or equipment. Once you gain proficiency, it is ideal to run through the obstacle course in your full combat equipment, carrying a weapon. Not only will this make the obstacle course more realistic and difficult, but it will help you test the setup of your equipment. For example, if the placement of a pouch makes it difficult for you to climb over a wall, you might need to reposition the pouch.

- You can run through the obstacle course as an individual or you can run through with a partner or a team. The technique for climbing over a wall alone is different from the technique for climbing over a wall with the help of teammates. Therefore, it is helpful to practice both techniques since you may end up applying both in real operations.

CLIMBING, SWIMMING AND WATER SURVIVAL

General Guidance

For alpine and maritime units, climbing, swimming and water survival are highly specialized skills that are beyond the scope of this book. However, climbing and swimming can still provide a great workout or cross-training activity for any tactical unit. Below are a few general concepts and suggestions for incorporating climbing, swimming and water survival into your combat fitness routine.

- Climbing can be a very useful skill in combat. If you are part of an alpine unit or urban assault unit, climbing may be a critical component of your training routine. If this is the case, you will probably want to build a high level of proficiency in climbing technique. You should also master the use of ropes and other climbing equipment in varying weather conditions.

- In other cases, it is useful to at least build some basic climbing ability in case you find yourself in a situation where you need to climb up or down a wall or rock face. For building basic climbing skills, a regular commercial climbing gym will probably be sufficient and you will not need to become a trained mountain climber. Some climbing and bouldering walls are very close to the ground, allowing you to get a good workout without needing complicated rope or belay systems.

- The nature of your swimming workout will largely depend on your mission requirements. At the very least, knowing how to swim is a critical combat skill. There are many situations where you might fall into deep water and need to swim to survive. In some cases, you might need to swim long distances to get to dry land.

- Swimming is also a very effective, low-impact total-body workout that can help build strength and cardiovascular endurance. Even if your operational requirements do not emphasize a need for swimming, swimming is a good cross-training option when trying to reduce impact on the joints from running and rucking.

- If you are swimming primarily for fitness, the principles for planning swimming workouts are similar to those for planning running workouts. You may conduct long distance swims, shorter distance timed swims, or sprint intervals. Learning to tread water for long periods can also be a good workout with numerous practical applications.

EXERCISE & TRAINING TECHNIQUES
Strength Training

It is best to choose strength exercises that build capabilities that will prove most useful in potential combat situations. For example, if you only conduct pull-ups with your own body weight, you might not be strong enough to climb onto a ledge in your gear when the time comes. The key is to train your muscles in the way they will most likely be used in combat.

In general, the best strength exercises for combat fitness are simple, functional movements that involve lifting, pulling and pushing. For combat fitness, it is generally better to pick exercises that challenge multiple muscle groups at one time and teach you to use muscles together in a coordinated manner.

Exercises that teach you to maintain balance, stabilize your core and generate force with your feet planted on the ground are also particularly useful. However, the more an exercise challenges your ability to balance and stabilize yourself, the greater the risk will be for injury. Many new trends in functional fitness incorporate greater instability into traditional exercises using tools like kettlebells, sandbags, unbalanced loads, elastic straps, balance boards and uneven surfaces etc. While this section focuses on demonstrating the most basic and stable forms of functional movements, it is possible to conduct any of the following exercises with less stable tools like kettlebells or sandbags. Always consider the risk of injury associated with more complex movements and master the technique for an exercise first before introducing instability.

Finally, this section provides only a few examples of strength training exercises and leaves out many well-known and effective exercises. We selected the exercises in this section either because they were useful for a wide range of tactical athletes, because they were less well-known or because they emphasize a particular concept of biomechanics or strength training. Therefore, we highly recommend that you learn and apply other exercises besides the limited selection provided here.

CORE STRENGTH EXERCISES

Biomechanics and Principles

When developing a strength training program, it makes sense to begin by focusing on core strength. Core strength is an essential component of all other exercises and strength training movements. Learning to use your core muscles properly will help you to perform exercises in a biomechanically correct manner. While traditional core exercises like sit-ups and crunches are still useful, they do not reflect how your core muscles are actually supposed to work in a functional or athletic context. For example, sit-ups entail bending at the waist and using your abdominal muscles to flex the upper body forwards at the hips. This is not a very common or practical movement and you will rarely use your abdominal muscles in this way except when you are doing sit-ups. Instead, most of the time you use your core muscles to stabilize your center of gravity while your arms and legs are running, changing direction, lifting, pushing or pulling. Therefore, in most athletic movements, the core muscles have a more static, stabilization or rotation role. The points below outline the fundamental concepts of how the core muscles are supposed to work and how to build core strength in the optimal way.

- To better understand how your core works, lie on your back with your legs straight. Place your hands on your ribcage and focus on your chest and lower back. You will probably notice that your lower back is raised off the floor and your ribcage is sticking up slightly. Now bend your knees and feel the change. Your lower back should sink towards the floor and your ribcage should collapse inward. Repeat the movement several times and focus on the sensations associated with bending the knees.

- After moving your legs from straight to bent several times, bend your legs but this time try to intensify the tightening of your ribcage and drop your sternum (chest) towards the floor. After practicing this exaggerated movement repeatedly, you will find a "neutral" position where your core feels tight, stable and comfortable. With repeated practice, you will begin to feel more comfortable with your core in this neutral position. The neutral position is the starting point for all of the following core exercises.

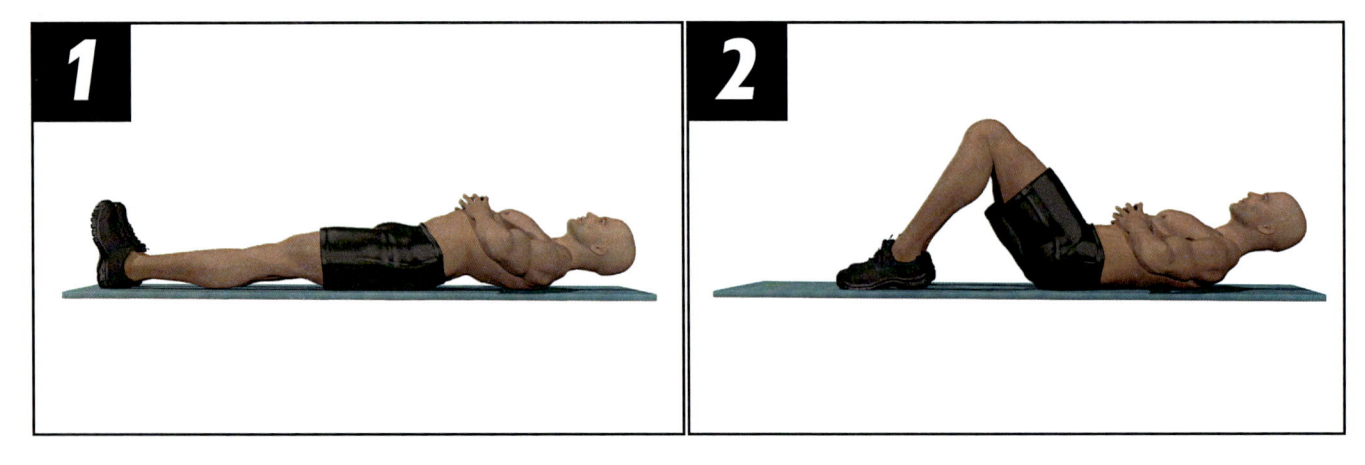

STRENGTH TRAINING

CORE STRENGTH EXERCISES

Unilateral Dumbbell Raise

The unilateral dumbbell raise helps you learn to use your core for stability while your arms and legs are moving and applying force in different directions. The challenge of the exercise is not in using the core muscles to move, but rather to use the core muscles to maintain the neutral position while the other limbs are moving. Be sure to conduct the movement with each arm.

1 START POSITION: Lie on your back in the neutral position with the knees bent. Place an approximately 8-inch ball or pillow between your knees and raise your legs approximately 10 inches off the ground, keeping your knees slightly bent. While raising your legs off the ground, try to keep your core in the neutral position. This should apply significant strain on your core muscles. You can place your freehand on your chest or abdomen.

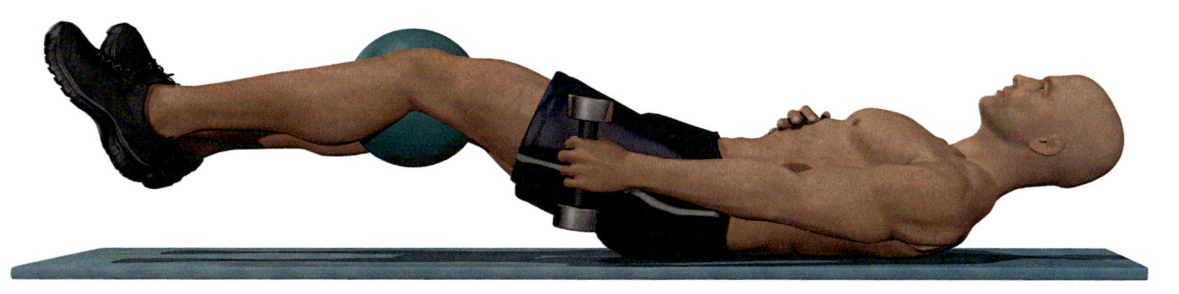

2 DUMBBELL RAISE: Hold a 5-pound dumbbell in one hand, even with your thigh. Exhale as you bring the dumbbell up in a wide arc until your arm is extended over your head. While you conduct this movement, focus on keeping your core neutral and your legs 10 inches off the ground.

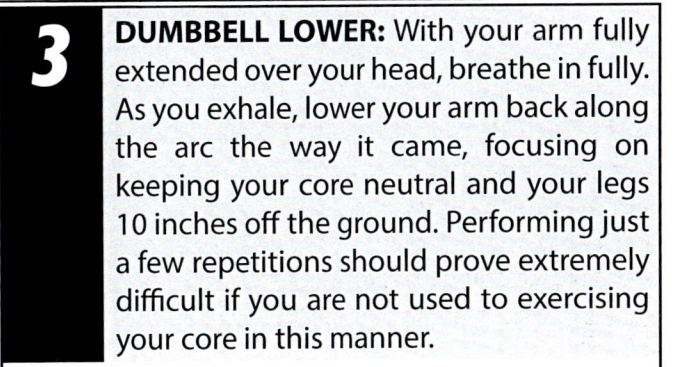

3 DUMBBELL LOWER: With your arm fully extended over your head, breathe in fully. As you exhale, lower your arm back along the arc the way it came, focusing on keeping your core neutral and your legs 10 inches off the ground. Performing just a few repetitions should prove extremely difficult if you are not used to exercising your core in this manner.

CORE STRENGTH EXERCISES

Bilateral Medicine Ball Raise

The bilateral medicine ball raise is similar to the unilateral dumbbell raise except you are applying force with both arms to move a medicine ball up and down along the arc instead of a single dumbbell. The bilateral movement can also be executed with elastic bands tied to an anchor point above your head as you lie down.

1 START POSITION: Lie on your back in the neutral position with the knees bent. Place an approximately 8-inch ball or pillow between your knees and raise your legs approximately 10 inches off the ground, keeping your knees slightly bent. While raising your legs off the ground, try to keep your core in the neutral position. This should apply significant strain on your core muscles.

2 MEDICINE BALL LOWER: Grasp the medicine ball and hold it above your head with your arms fully extended. Exhale as you bring the ball down in a wide arc until the ball touches your thighs. While you conduct this movement, focus on keeping your core neutral and your legs 10 inches off the ground.

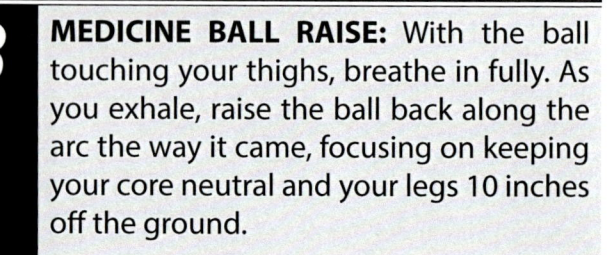

3 MEDICINE BALL RAISE: With the ball touching your thighs, breathe in fully. As you exhale, raise the ball back along the arc the way it came, focusing on keeping your core neutral and your legs 10 inches off the ground.

CORE STRENGTH EXERCISES

Other Exercises

While it is best to perform exercises that teach the core to provide stability for other movements, more traditional core exercises can also be useful. However, some exercises are better than others in terms of the benefits they provide for performance and functional movement. Four such exercises are explained below.

SIDE BENDS: Stand upright with your feet together and your hands on your hips. While attempting to keep yourself completely stationary below the waist, bend the torso to the left and right in smooth, quick movements.

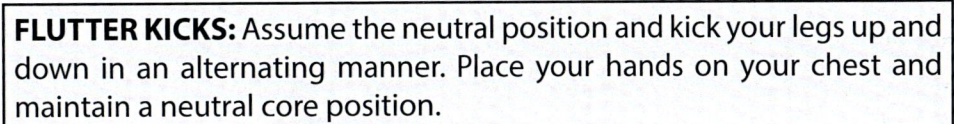

FLUTTER KICKS: Assume the neutral position and kick your legs up and down in an alternating manner. Place your hands on your chest and maintain a neutral core position.

BICYCLE: Assume the neutral position and place your hands touching the sides of your head. Alternate touching your right elbow to your left knee and your left elbow to your right knee.

PLANKS: Assume the push-up position (on either your hands or elbows) and keep your body as straight as possible for a set period of time. You can also conduct planks with your back or side facing the ground to exercise the obliques or lower back.

BODY WEIGHT EXERCISES

Push-Ups

Body weight training is one of the most effective and versatile training methods but is frequently underappreciated because of increasing focus on weight training. One of the biggest advantages of body weight training is that you can do it anywhere, without the need for expensive equipment. One of the most common body weight exercises is the push-up. As a tactical athlete, it is preferable to conduct the push-up on your knuckles or fingertips. Not only does this place less strain on the wrists but it can also help build finger strength, forearm strength and punching ability for empty-hand fighting. It is best to perform push-ups in a controlled manner, through your full range of motion.

1 START POSITION: Choose either the fist or finger-tip push-up and place both hands on the ground with the feet close together and the body straight.

2 LOWER: Lower your chest to the ground in a smooth motion, keeping the body straight and the elbows close to your body.

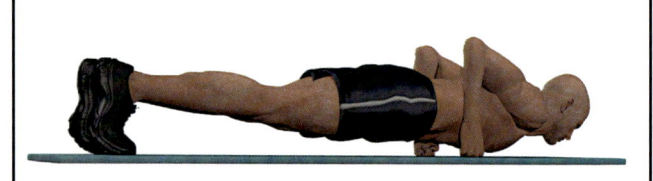

3 PUSH: Push with your arms to raise your body back to the start position. Ensure to keep your elbows in and your body straight the entire time.

BODY WEIGHT EXERCISES

Pull-Ups

Pull-ups are another extremely effective exercise. You do not necessarily need a pull-up bar to perform pull-ups. You can use any sturdy ledge or sill. Sometimes, picking a smaller ledge can help improve finger strength and climbing ability. In addition, even when using a bar, as a tactical athlete it is better to use a "thumbs over" grip, similar to the grip you would use to pull yourself up onto a ledge. Variations to make the exercise harder include performing pull-ups with your body in an L-shape, legs extended in front of you, or pulling yourself up until the bar is even with your waist (also called a muscle-up).

1 START POSITION: Grasp the bar or ledge with your thumbs wrapped over the top. Make sure to hang with the arms fully extended.

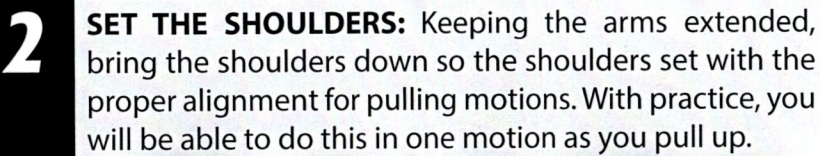

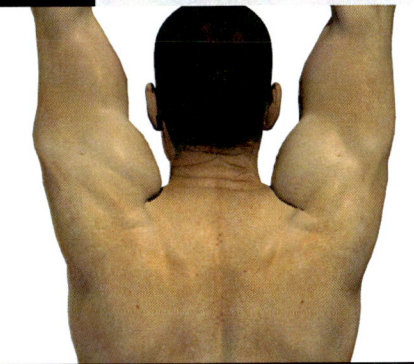

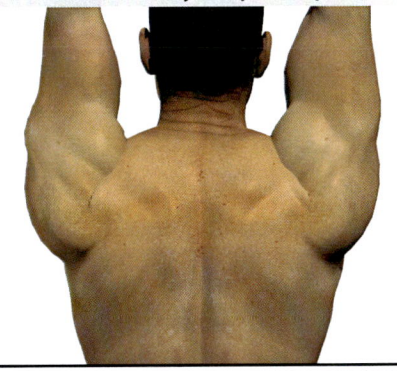

2 SET THE SHOULDERS: Keeping the arms extended, bring the shoulders down so the shoulders set with the proper alignment for pulling motions. With practice, you will be able to do this in one motion as you pull up.

3 PULL UP: Pull yourself up, squeezing the shoulder blades together as you pull. Ideally you should attempt to touch the bar to your upper chest. Then lower yourself back down letting the arms extend fully and then letting the shoulders rise back up so you are hanging relaxed.

FREE WEIGHT EXERCISES

Deadlift (1 of 2)

The deadlift builds strength in one of the most common functional movements you may need to perform on the battlefield, lifting a heavy object off the ground. As a tactical athlete, it is generally better to perform the deadlift rather than the squat since in a real combat situation, resistance will more likely be in your hands as opposed to on your shoulders if you need to perform a squat motion. In addition, the deadlift forces you to perform the squat with better form. Avoid using a belt if possible since you will not have a belt in a combat situation and it is important to learn to use your core to keep your body in the right posture.

1 **START POSITION:** Place the feet approximately shoulder-width apart and squat down to grasp the bar with an overhand/underhand grip, hands spaced slightly wider than your feet. Your knees should not come forward; your hips should be as far back as possible and your back should be straight but bent forward at the waist so your chest is over the bar. Your head and neck should be relaxed and aligned with your spine.

FREE WEIGHT EXERCISES

Deadlift (2 of 2)

2 **PUSH THROUGH THE FEET:** Push through the feet, keeping the hips back and preventing the knees from coming forward. When you are learning the movement, you may need to push through the heels in order to keep the knees back. The bar should raise straight up, clearing your knees as your back straightens. It is important to use the legs and not the back to lift the weight.

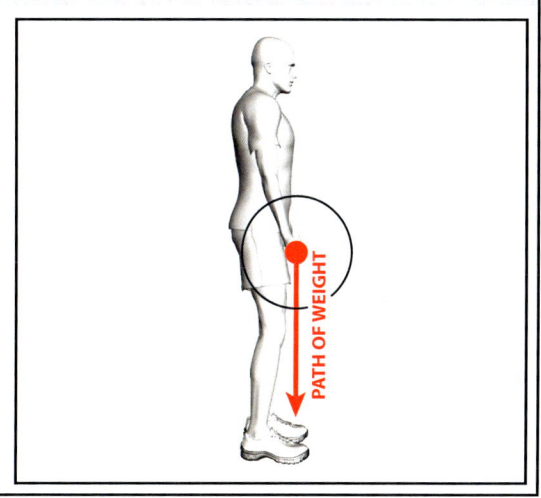

3 **LOWER THE WEIGHT:** Lower the weight back straight down, clearing your knees. Lead the motion by driving your hips back and down, keeping your knees from coming forward. It is important not to bend over at the waist but instead initiate the movement by driving the hips down and back.

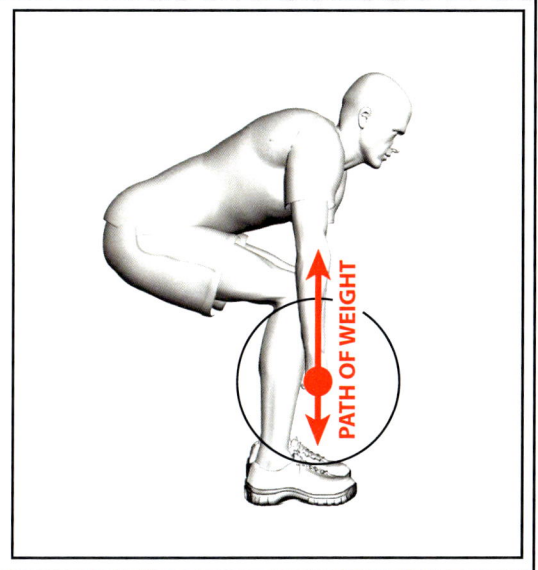

FREE WEIGHT EXERCISES

Step-Up (1 of 2)

The step-up uses a similar movement as the deadlift. When conducting the step-up, it is very easy to perform the motion improperly by pushing off with your toe to raise yourself up onto the step. Using the correct form calls for lifting yourself onto the step entirely with the stepping leg, without letting the knee come forward. To do this you must drive through the stepping leg in a smooth, controlled motion. Always ensure you have a firm grip on the weights so you do not drop them.

1 START POSITION: Hold a weight in each hand and face a step, approximately 12 inches high. Step with one foot onto the step. lean forward so your weight is over your stepping foot without letting your stepping knee come forward.

2 STEP UP: Push through your stepping foot to raise yourself up. Do not let the stepping knee come forward and do not push off with your rear foot. To ensure you do not push off, it can help to let your toe be the first part of your rear foot to leave the ground.

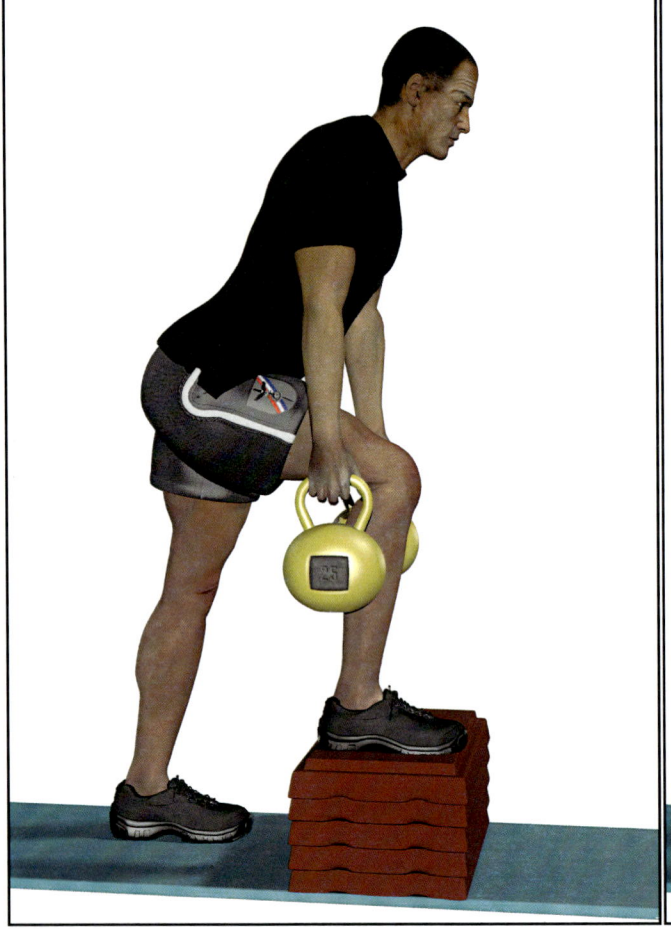

FREE WEIGHT EXERCISES

Step-Up (2 of 2)

3 **STAND ON THE STEP:** Bring both feet onto the step and stand tall with good posture, preparing to lower your foot back to the ground.

4 **LOWER THE FOOT:** Step backwards and slowly lower the foot back to the ground using the same motion you used to step-up, except in reverse. Keep the knee back and the back straight as you step down. You can either step up with the same foot each time or alternate feet.

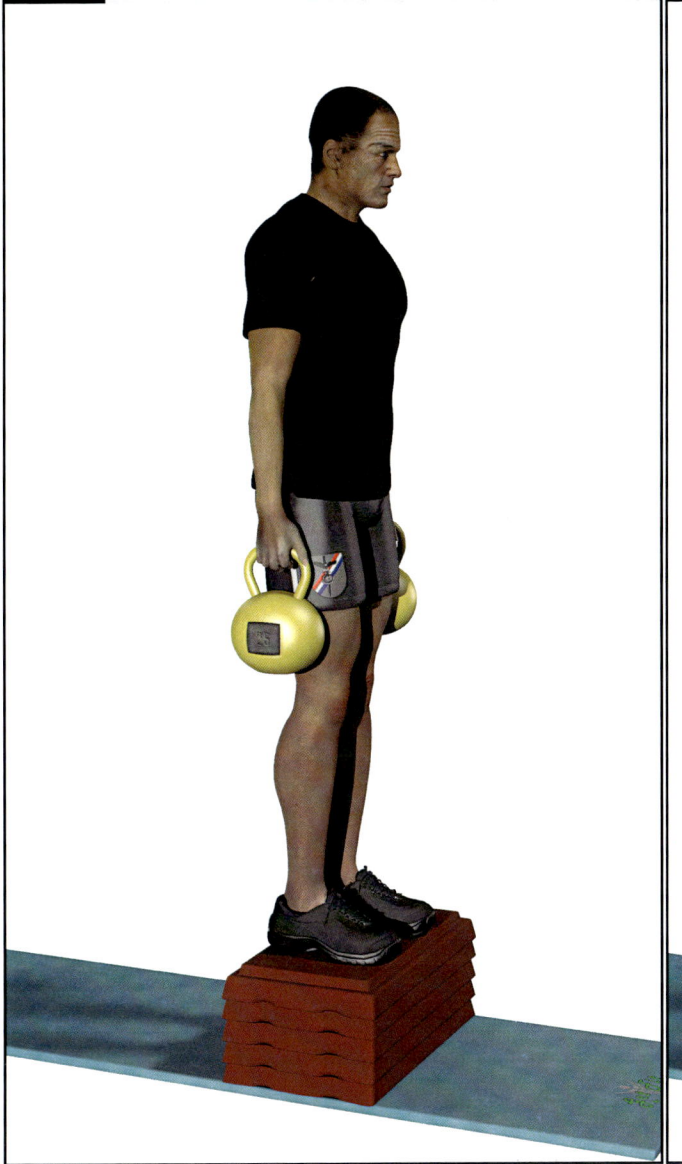

FREE WEIGHT EXERCISES

Posterior Lunge (1 of 2)

The posterior lunge helps develop the correct lunge form. Once you master the posterior lunge you can move on to walking lunges and other lunge combinations. The mechanics of the lunge are similar to those used for the deadlift and step-up. The steps below separate the drive through the rear leg and the drive through the front leg. However, with practice you should perform the complete lunge as one motion.

1 STEP BACK INTO THE LUNGE: Start with the feet together, holding dumbbells in the hands. Step backwards onto your toe and then lower your back knee towards the ground, keeping your front knee from moving forward.

2 DRIVE THROUGH THE REAR LEG: While keeping your front knee from coming forward, push through the rear toe, fully extending the back leg.

FREE WEIGHT EXERCISES

Posterior Lunge (2 of 2)

3 DRIVE THROUGH THE FRONT LEG: After driving through the rear leg, your weight should be fully over your front leg. Drive through the front leg without letting the front knee come forward just as you did in the step-up movement.

4 RETURN TO START POSITION: Driving through the front leg will allow you to bring the rear foot back to the front foot. You can repeat the movement multiple times to complete your set, either using the same leg or alternating legs.

FREE WEIGHT EXERCISES

Bench Press (1 of 2)

The bench press is one of the most functional and effective free weight exercises for the upper body. The bench press improves your ability to push heavy objects or lift an object off of your chest in an emergency. As a tactical athlete, it is generally preferable to use a slightly narrower grip (about shoulder-width apart) than the common bench press grip. This is because, in a real-life situation, you will probably need to generate pushing force closer to your centerline.

1 **GRIP THE BAR:** Lie on the bench and grip the bar with your hands approximately shoulder-width apart. When conducting the exercise, try to prevent from arching your back and letting it come too far off the bench.

2 **LOWER:** Start with the bar even with your eyes. Lower the bar to your chest, keeping your elbows in. As the bar comes down it should move slightly in the direction of your feet, making contact with your chest just below your pectoral muscles. Inhale as the bar lowers.

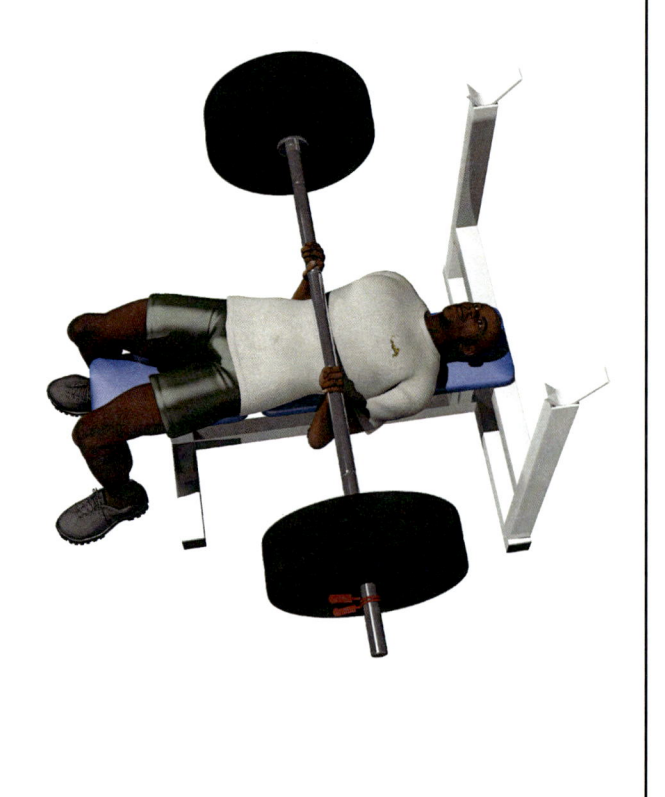

FREE WEIGHT EXERCISES

Bench Press (2 of 2)

3 **PRESS:** As you push the bar back up, it should travel back towards your head so it ends in a position even with your eyes. Keep your elbows in while extending the bar upward and exhale while extending.

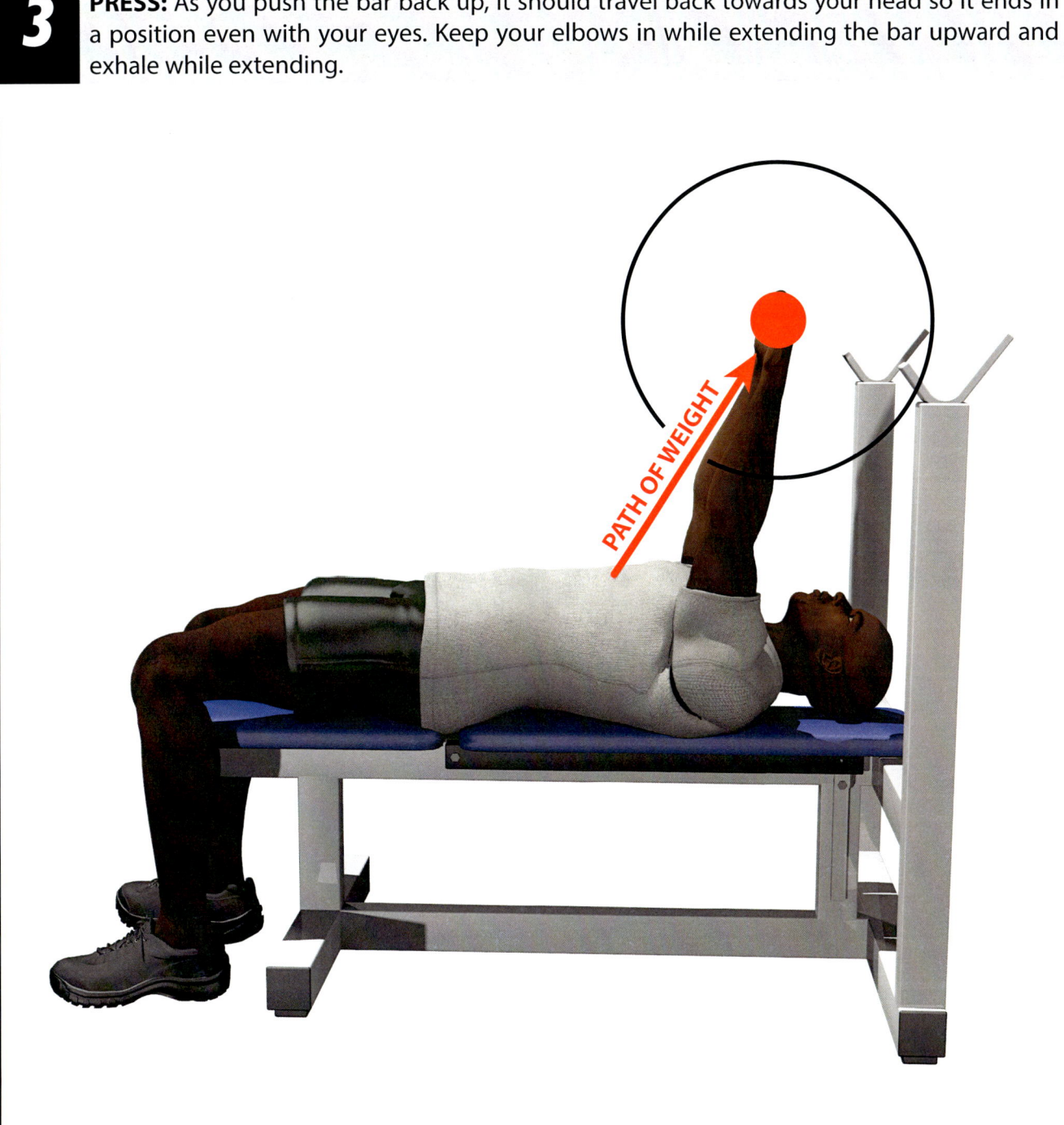

FREE WEIGHT EXERCISES

One-Arm Overhead Press (1 of 2)

For the tactical athlete, it is useful to be able to generate force over the head with one hand. A one-handed overhead press is more challenging than a two-handed press since it forces you to use your core and stabilizer muscles to support the unbalanced weight. If you practice the one-arm overhead press you will be ready to generate lifting force above your head with one arm if needed in a combat situation because your other hand is occupied.

1   **STARTING POSITION:** Sit upright and hold the dumbbell about even with your ear. The most critical part of the movement is making sure not to hunch your shoulder and instead keeping the trapezius muscle relaxed. To do this drive the shoulder down and away from the ear so the shoulder joint is set correctly for the lifting motion. It will take some practice to learn to relax the trapezius muscle. You can poke the trapezius muscle to see if it is relaxed.

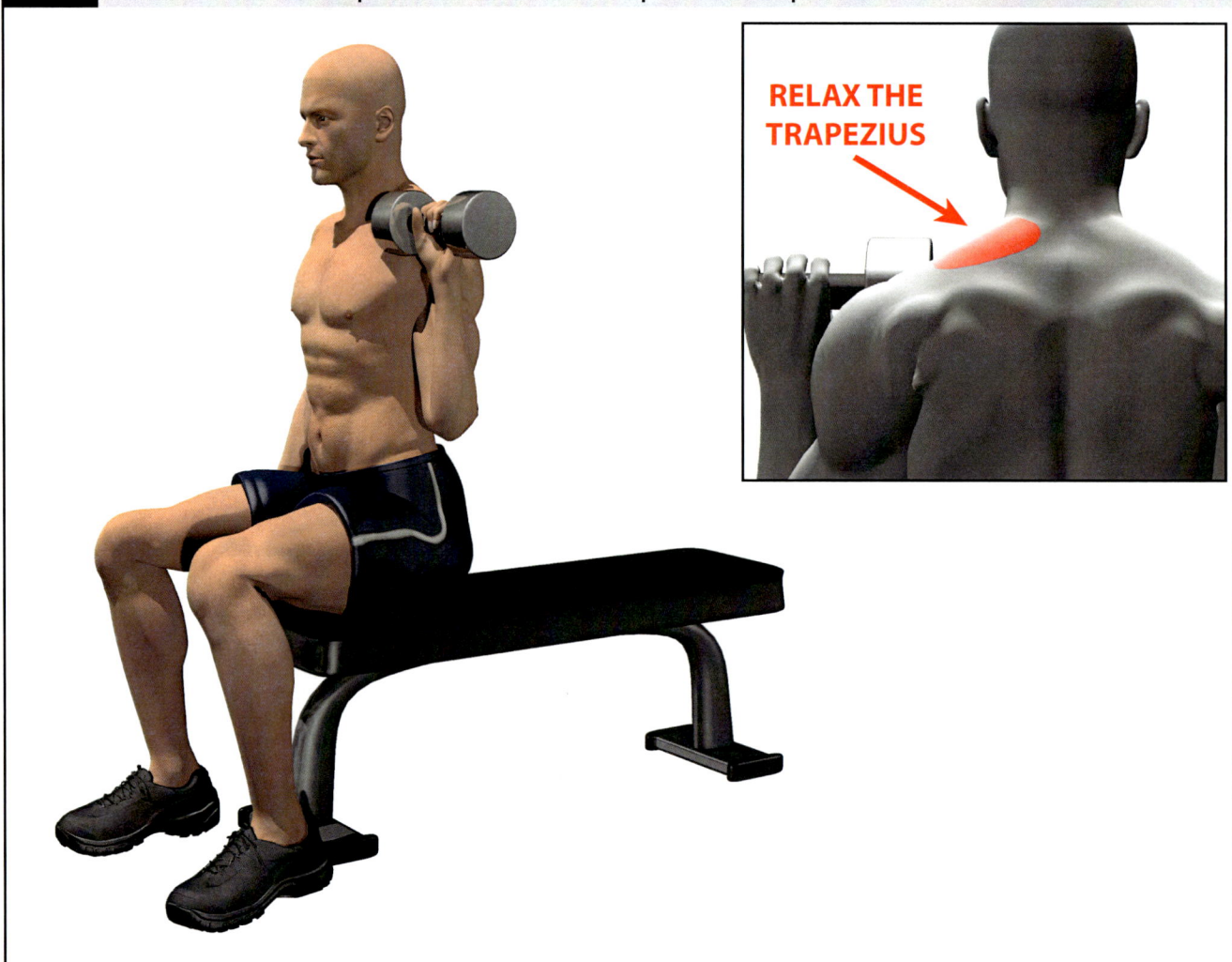

RELAX THE TRAPEZIUS

FREE WEIGHT EXERCISES

One-Arm Overhead Press (2 of 2)

2 **DRIVE UPWARD:** Keeping the trapezius muscle relaxed, drive the weight upward until your arm is straight up. When you do this correctly your shoulder will not hunch and you will feel your scapula (shoulder blade) rotating down and out as your arm extends upwards.

3 **LOWER:** Lower the weight in the same way you lifted it, keeping the trapezius relaxed.

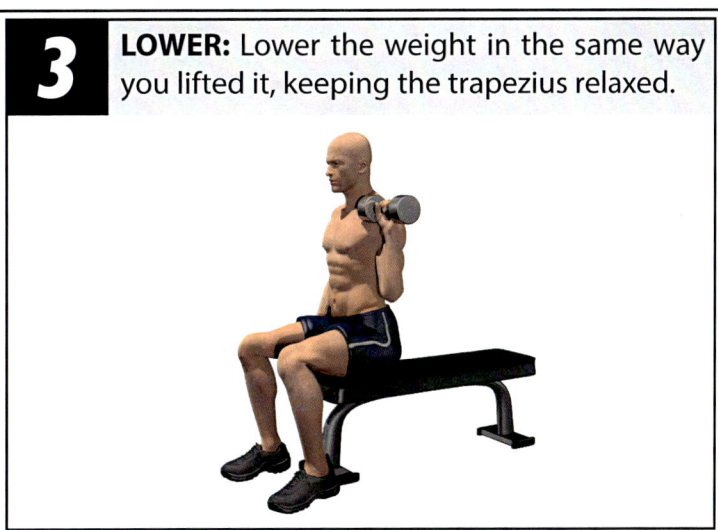

FREE WEIGHT EXERCISES

One-Arm Row (1 of 2)

As with the one-arm overhead press, for the tactical athlete, it is useful to be able to generate pulling force with one hand. There are many combat situations where you may need to pull with one hand, for example, you may need to pull a buddy upward onto the roof of a building. The one-arm dumbbell row does not just build pulling strength but it also builds the core and stabilizer muscles that allow you to generate maximum force with one hand.

1 STARTING POSITION: Place one knee on a bench and the other leg on the ground in a partial squat posture, using the same squat form used for the deadlift. Lean forward and place one hand at eye level on the bench and grasp the dumbbell with the other hand. Your back should be straight and your arm should be fully extended with the dumbbell hanging.

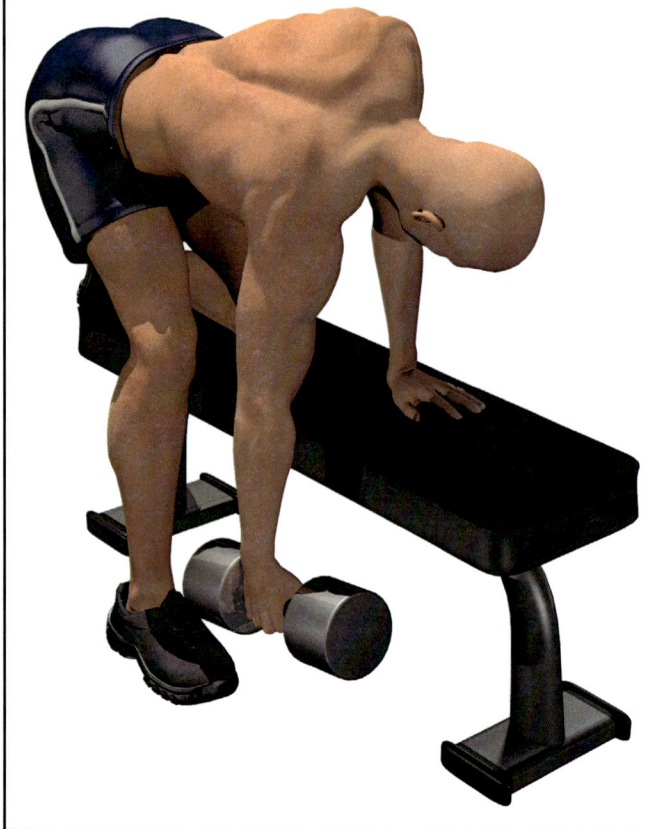

2 SET THE SHOULDER: Before pulling the dumbbell up, first set the shoulder by bringing it back towards the ceiling and squeezing the shoulder blades slightly. The weight should continue to hang as you set the shoulder. In the beginning, you may have to set the shoulder and then lift. With practice, you will be able to do one after the other in one movement.

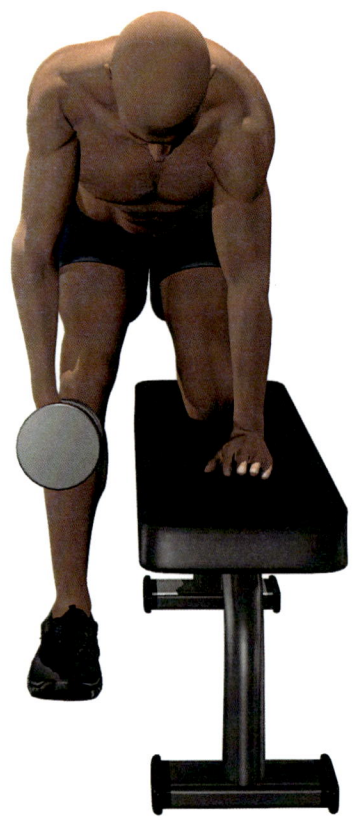

FREE WEIGHT EXERCISES

One-Arm Row (2 of 2)

3 **LIFT:** Lift the weight upward, keeping the shoulder set. The weight should travel in a slight rearward direction, stopping at a point near your hip.

4 **LOWER:** Lower the weight back down in the same way it came up. Once your arm is fully extended, let the shoulder slide forward, out of the set position, to achieve full extension.

CABLE EXERCISES

Four-Way Hip (1 of 2)

Using a cable machine to conduct single-leg hip extension, flexion, abduction and adduction is a great way to build functional hip strength while improving balance and stability. Ultimately, when generating force with the hips, it is critical to remain firmly grounded and balanced. For the four-way hip exercise, you will stand on a small block with one leg and attach the cable to your other leg with an ankle cuff. You can then conduct the four-way movement with the cable (either machine or elastic) providing the resistance. Ideally, you should balance on the base leg and not hold onto anything. As you improve, you can stand on a half foam-roller or balance board instead of a block to make the balancing exercise even harder.

EXTENSION: Face the cable machine and extend the leg to the rear and up to about a 30-degree angle while keeping the leg straight.	**FLEXION:** Face away from the cable machine and extend the leg forward and up to about a 30-degree angle while keeping the leg straight.

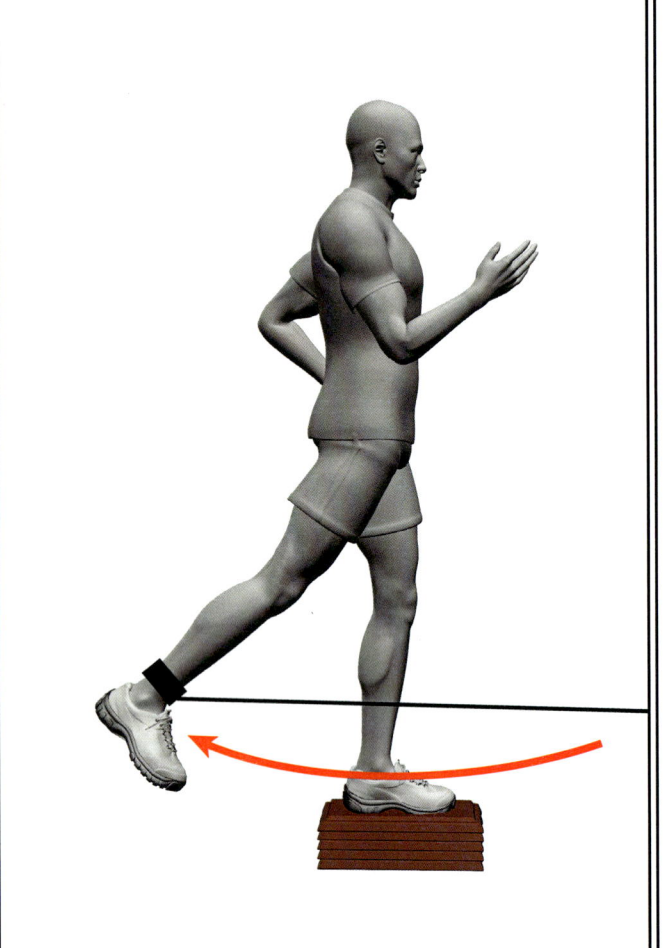

CABLE EXERCISES

Four-Way Hip (2 of 2)

ABDUCTION: Position yourself with the machine to the opposite side of the working leg. Start with the feet together and then extend the leg out sideways to about a 30-degree angle.

ADDUCTION: Position yourself with the machine to the same side as the working leg. Let the resistance pull the working leg out and up until it is at about a 30-degree angle. Bring the leg inward so your heel is touching the toe of the base leg and then let it move back out to the 30-degree angle starting position.

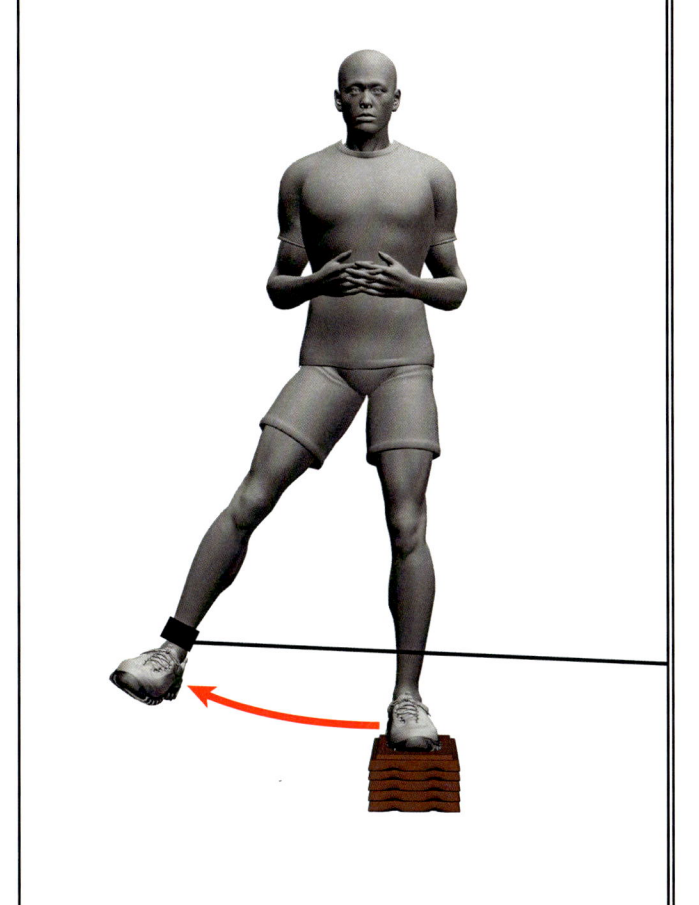

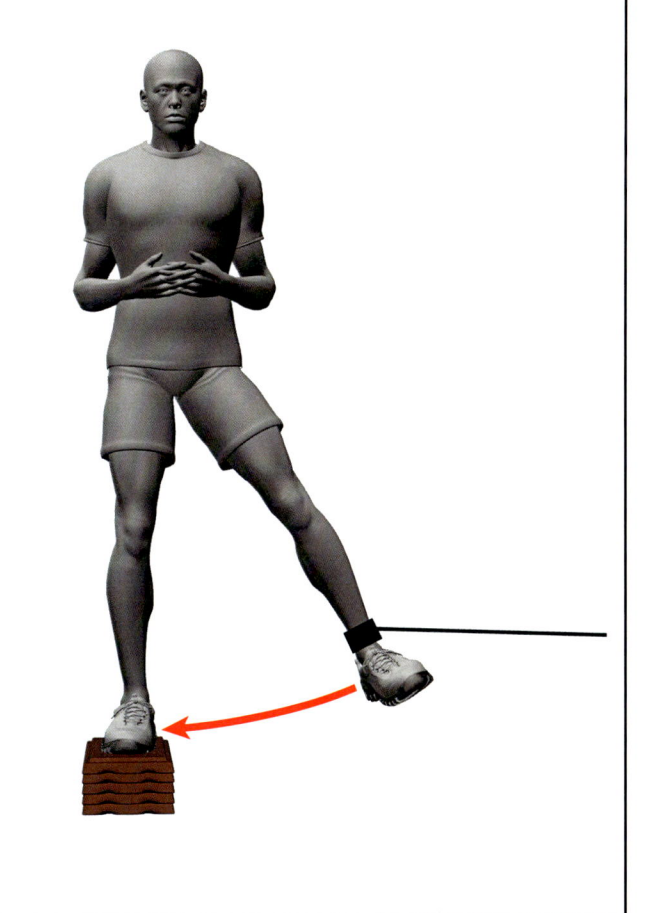

CABLE EXERCISES

One-Arm Lateral Row (1 of 2)

Using a cable machine to perform the lateral row not only strengthens the arms and back but it also forces you to generate force by rotating your hips and torso while keeping your legs firmly planted on the ground. The ability to generate lateral force with the feet planted on the ground is a common, functional movement and can prove useful in a variety of combat situations. For ease of explanation, the example below explains how to conduct the exercise with the right hand.

1 STARTING POSITION: Set the level of the cable just below the shoulder and grasp the handle with the right hand. Place the left foot forward and the right foot back and let the right arm extend as far forward as possible as the torso rotates to the left.

2 SET THE SHOULDER: As you move your shoulder back into the set position, rotate the hips and torso to the right.

CABLE EXERCISES

One-Arm Lateral Row (2 of 2)

3 **PULL BACK:** Once the shoulder is set, continue to pull back until your right hand is flush with the side of your body. Continue to rotate to pull the cable as far as possible.

4 **RESET:** Let the cable move forward the way it came, rotating to the left as the shoulder comes out of the set position to achieve full extension.

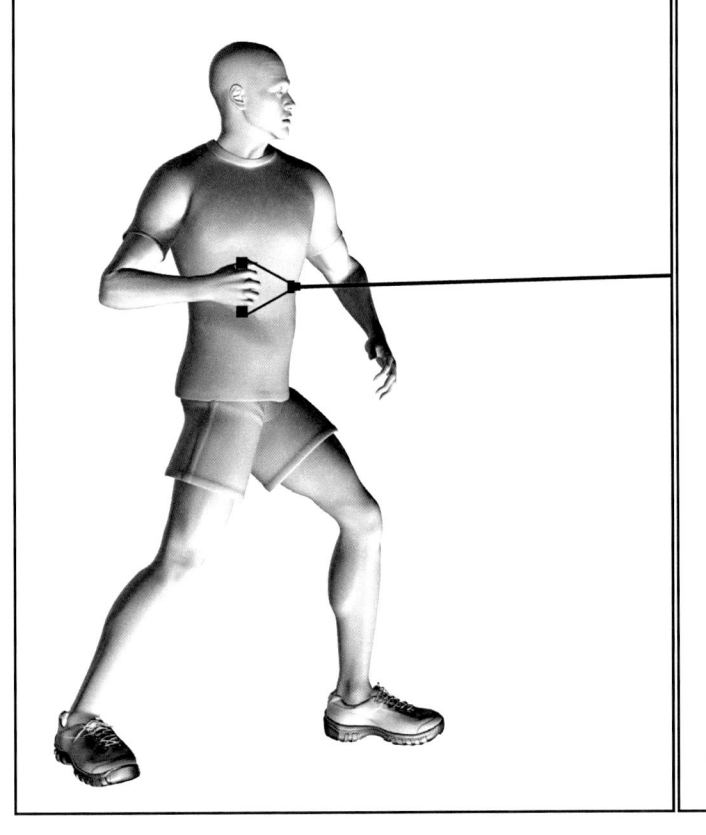

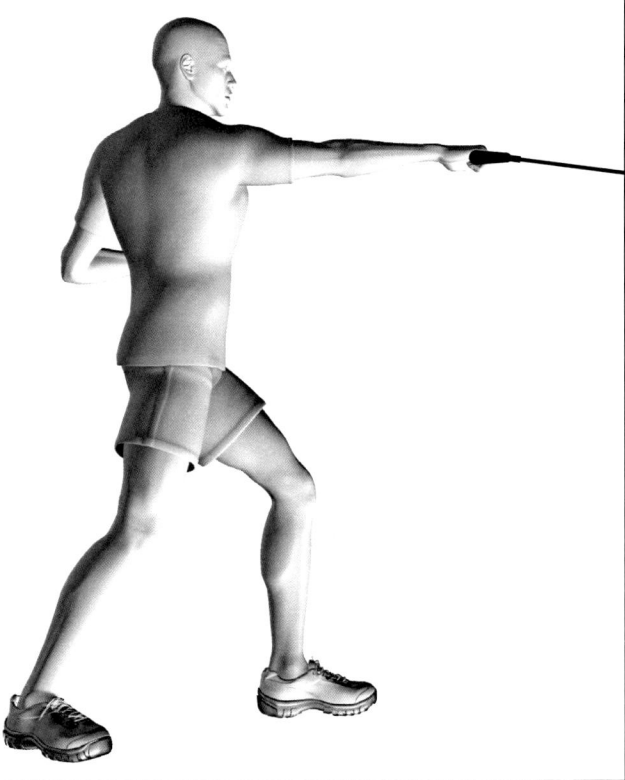

CABLE EXERCISES

Reverse Wood Chopper (1 of 2)

The reverse wood chopper is a particularly good exercise for the tactical athlete because it combines many of the movements from the exercises already described into a single, total-body movement. The movement starts with a deadlift, incorporates the rotation from the cable row and ends with a similar movement as the single-arm shoulder press.

1 STARTING POSITION: Begin standing on a box with the cable below you to one side. Squat down in the proper squat form and grasp the handle of the cable with both hands in whatever way feels comfortable to you.

2 ROTATE AND LIFT: Bring the cable up and across your body as you stand up using correct deadlift form. Rotate the body away from the cable as you bring the cable up across your chest, keeping it close to your body.

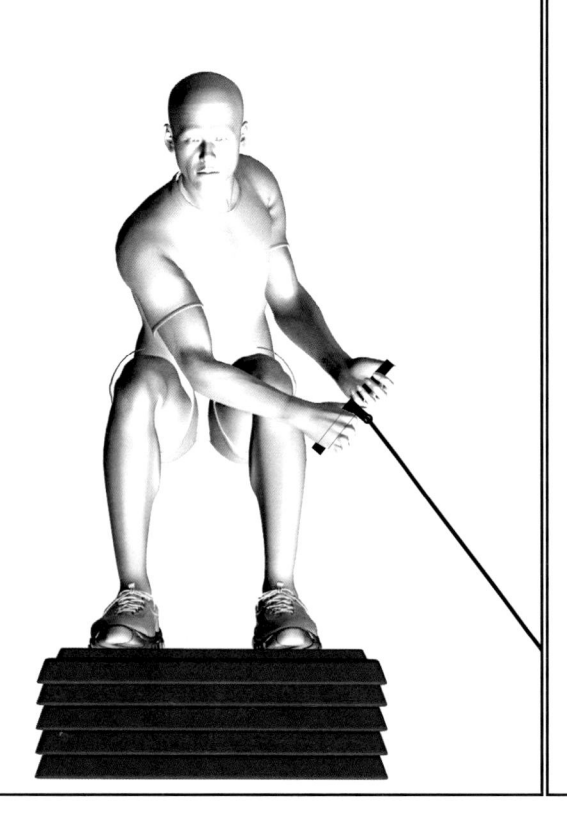

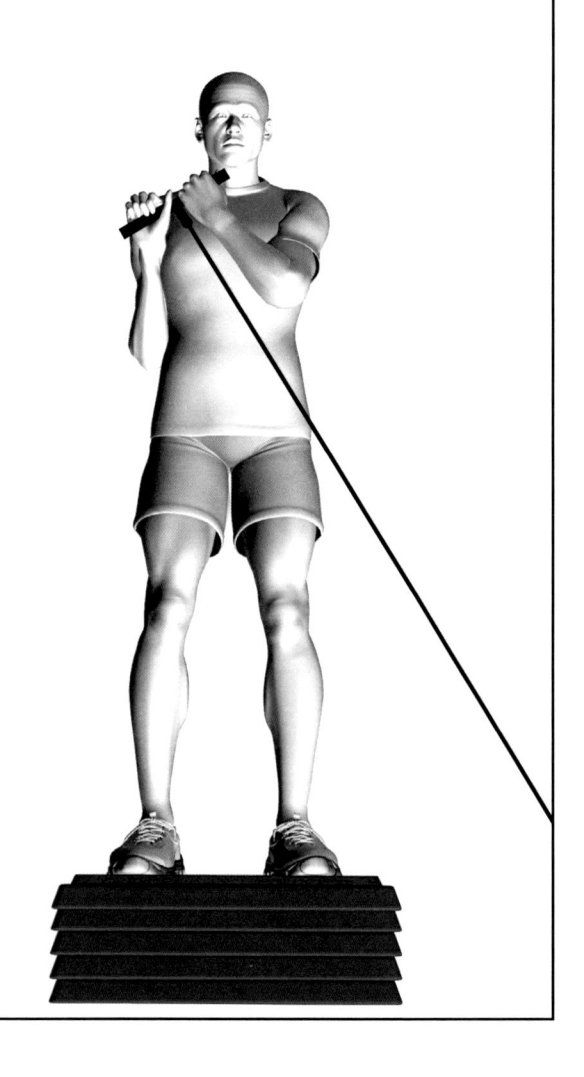

CABLE EXERCISES

Reverse Wood Chopper (2 of 2)

3 **OVERHEAD PRESS:** As the cable comes up across your body, continue to rotate and lift the cable above the head, achieving a near full extension with both arms.

4 **RESET:** Rotate in the opposite direction as you bring the cable back down the way it came and squat into the starting position.

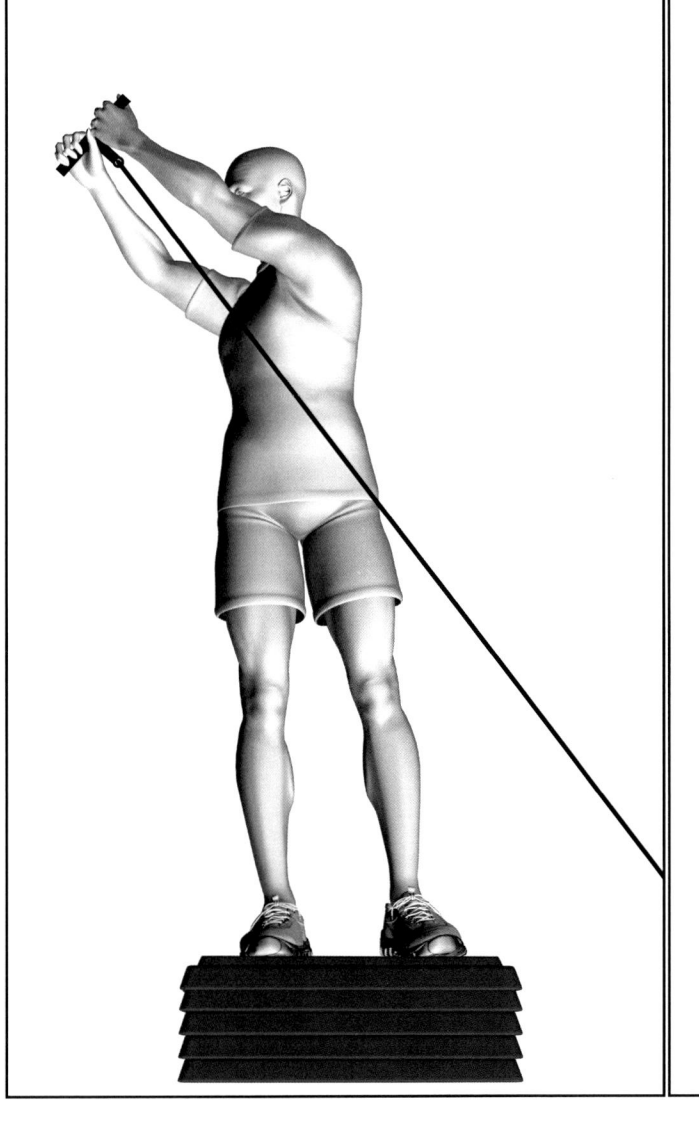

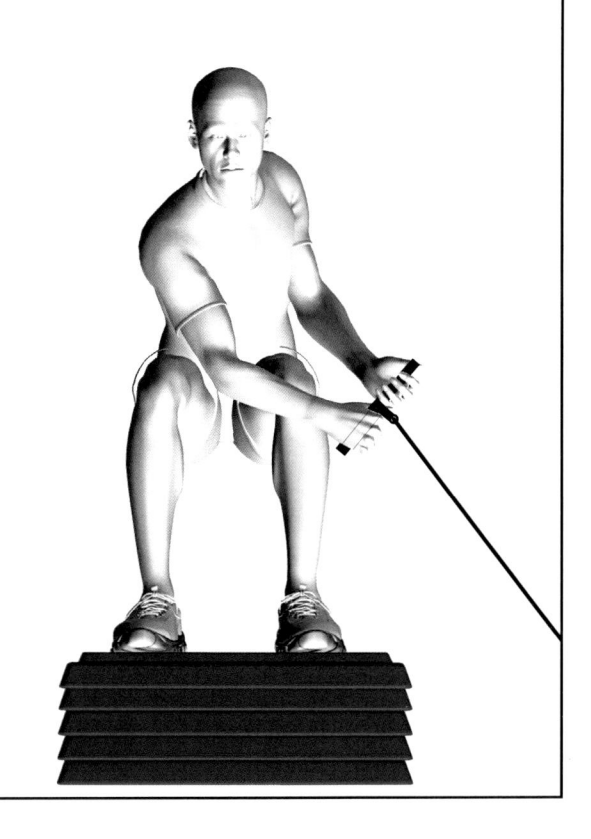

EXERCISE & TRAINING TECHNIQUES
Balance, Coordination and Dexterity

For combat fitness programs it is useful to choose exercises that place particular focus on balance, coordination and dexterity. In combat, it is critically important to be able to maintain your balance and manipulate objects with your hands in high-stress situations. Furthermore, you may be operating at night, in rough terrain or bad weather. Therefore, a high level of athletic coordination is critical for the combat athlete.

Many people's experience playing sports as children has reinforced a myth that certain people are born more coordinated than others and that there is little that can be done to change that. Genetics and natural ability are not nearly as important as most people believe. It is very possible for anyone to dramatically increase their coordination and athletic ability through training, practice and playing sports.

Martial arts training provides the same benefits as sports while also preparing you for unarmed combat on the battlefield and helping build an aggressive, fighter's mindset. Martial arts began as combative arts designed to help warriors win on the battlefield. Over time, many traditions moved away from the practical combat focus and transformed into more stylized disciplines for the purpose of hobby, sport or personal development. Recent trends in "mixed martial arts" have in some way returned to the original focus on practical fighting. However, modern mixed martial arts are in some cases still built around athletic competitions and require some modification for combat purposes.

One of the best options for martial arts training is to combine elements of modern mixed martial arts with elements of the original, ancient, combative martial arts. Almost all of the ancient combative arts incorporated weapons training. While we no longer use ancient weapons on the battlefield today, training with ancient weapons (the long stick in particular) still remains one of the most effective fitness tools for developing balance, coordination, dexterity, speed and endurance.

STICK TRAINING

Benefits of Martial Arts Fitness

When building balance, coordination and dexterity for functional movement, it is often best to train as many attributes at one time as possible, in order to replicate the demands of real combat. Stick training simultaneously improves balance, coordination, dexterity, endurance, strength, agility, foot speed, hand speed and grip strength. Stick training traces its roots to traditional martial arts systems of ancient warrior cultures such as the Spartans, Samurai and Vikings. Nearly all warrior cultures employed stick or spear training as a foundation for fitness and the fighting arts. There are many benefits of stick training for the modern combat athlete as well, including the following:

ENHANCED COMBAT SHOOTING: The movements used in martial arts stick training are the same movements used in combat shooting. For example, pivoting and striking with the stick uses the same muscles needed to rapidly pivot with the pistol or rifle to engage targets to the sides or rear. The hand speed, control, grip strength and shock absorption needed to strike with the stick carry over to help you manipulate a pistol or rifle faster, more precisely and control the recoil after firing.

ENHANCED SELF-DEFENSE: The movements used in martial arts stick training are also the same movements used in other self-defense and martial arts techniques. Learning to move quickly and smoothly with the stick will improve your skill and coordination when wielding a knife or tactical baton. Stick training will build your speed and power for performing strikes, throws and joint manipulations in empty-hand fighting.

OVERLOAD TRAINING: Because the stick is long, heavy and challenging to wield, practicing moving and fighting with the stick will provide a degree of "overload training" for weapons manipulation. Essentially, after getting used to manipulating the stick, manipulating the rifle, pistol, knife or baton will feel very easy in comparison.

LOW-IMPACT TOTAL BODY TRAINING: Stick training is one of the most versatile training systems for the combat athlete because it builds many skills and attributes simultaneously. Nearly every muscle is taxed when conducting stick drills, including smaller stabilizer muscles and the muscles in the hands and feet. In addition, stick drills place less strain on the joints than running or rucking.

STICK TRAINING

Fundamentals

When stood on its end, the stick should come somewhere between your armpit and your eyes. While it is possible to use a longer or shorter stick, this height range will provide the greatest versatility. You may also choose to use a lighter stick made out of bamboo or rattan, or a heavy stick made out of hickory or another hardwood. Lighter sticks are better for building speed while a heavier stick builds more strength. If you incorporate any striking into your routines, it is generally better to use a more durable hardwood to minimize the risk of the stick breaking and causing injury. While it is beyond the scope of this manual to discuss stick training in detail, many martial arts systems include stick training. Below are some general guidelines for incorporating stick training into your combat fitness workout.

FORM: Form training focuses on developing coordination. Conduct movements slowly, focusing on correct form. It can be helpful to film yourself to evaluate your form.

ENDURANCE: You can use stick training to build endurance by conducting repeated drills at a sustainable pace without any rest. With practice, it is possible to move continuously for over an hour.

SPEED: To build speed, perform drills as fast as possible and time the results, working towards faster and faster times.

INTERVALS: You can intensify the stick training workouts by performing speed or endurance intervals with prescribed rest periods, just as you would for a running routine.

STRIKING: Striking a bag or rubber target (like a tire) with the stick places a greater emphasis on power, grip strength and shock absorption.

STICK TRAINING

Four-Direction Drill (1 of 8)

There are an unlimited number of possible stick training drills and by studying martial arts you can learn existing drills and develop your ability to design your own. Below is one example of a drill that is easy to learn and incorporates simple functional movements. You do not need to spend years studying martial arts to reap the fitness benefits of stick training. Even incorporating the single drill below into your existing fitness program could help you make significant fitness gains. The sequence below can be repeated as many times as you would like. Since each sequence ends with a 90-degree turn, conducting them one after another will lead you to conduct the pattern in a complete circle (four directions) until you are facing the same direction you started in.

1 **STARTING POSITION:** Begin by holding the stick close to one end, with your hands about shoulder width apart, the right hand in front of the left hand. You should hold the stick near your waist and point it where an imaginary opponent's eyes would be. Your right foot should be forward and your knees slightly bent in a comfortable, fighter's stance.

FRONT

TOP

ANGLE

STICK TRAINING

Four-Direction Drill (2 of 8)

2 **JAB:** Shuffle forward slightly as you jab the stick forward in a strike to the head.

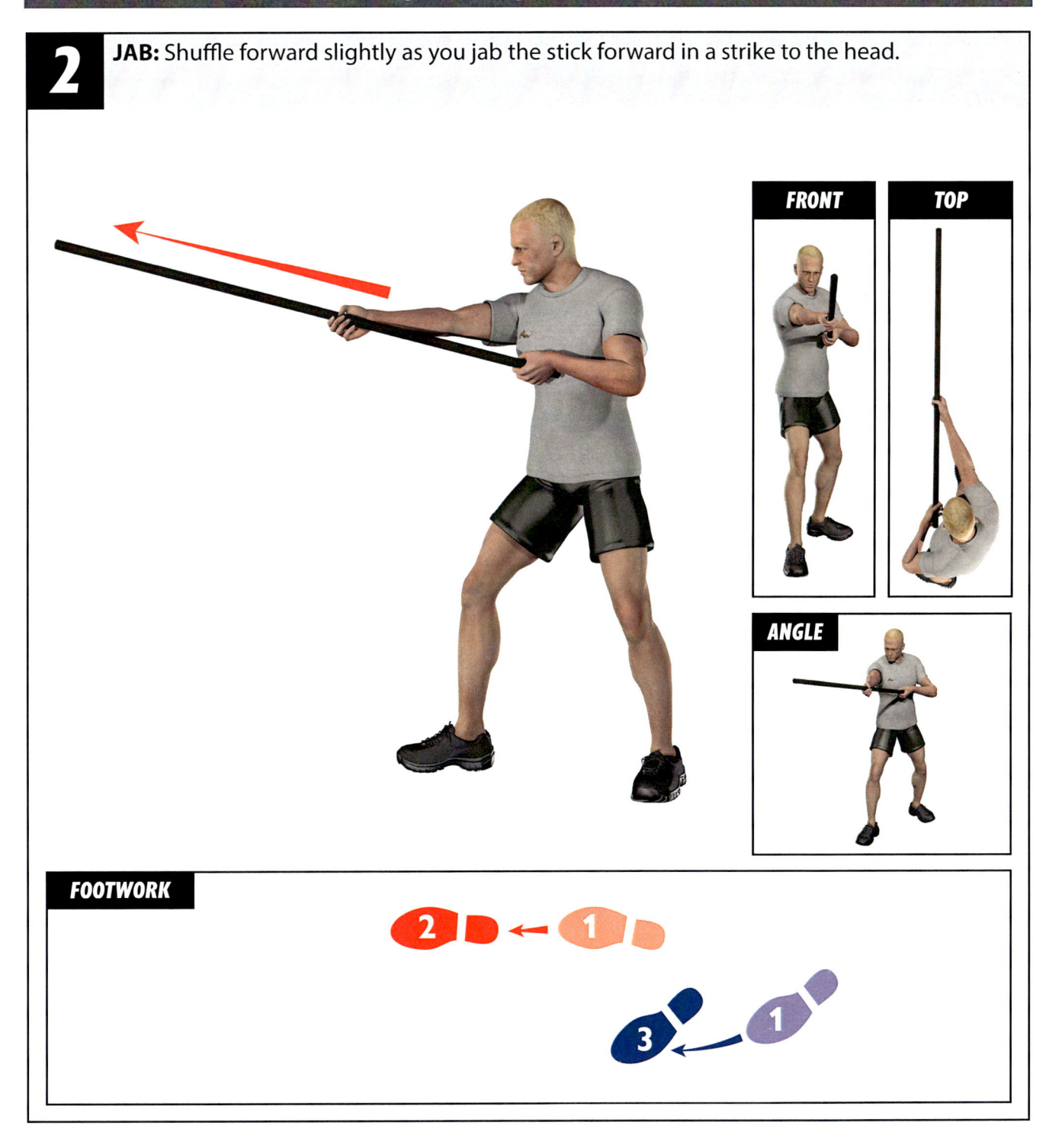

FRONT

TOP

ANGLE

FOOTWORK

STICK TRAINING

Four-Direction Drill (3 of 8)

3 **UNDER THE ARM:** Step back with the right leg as you swing the stick over your head in a counter-clockwise motion and then strike downward and to the right at a 45-degree angle. The stick should end up under your arm with the butt of the stick braced in the armpit.

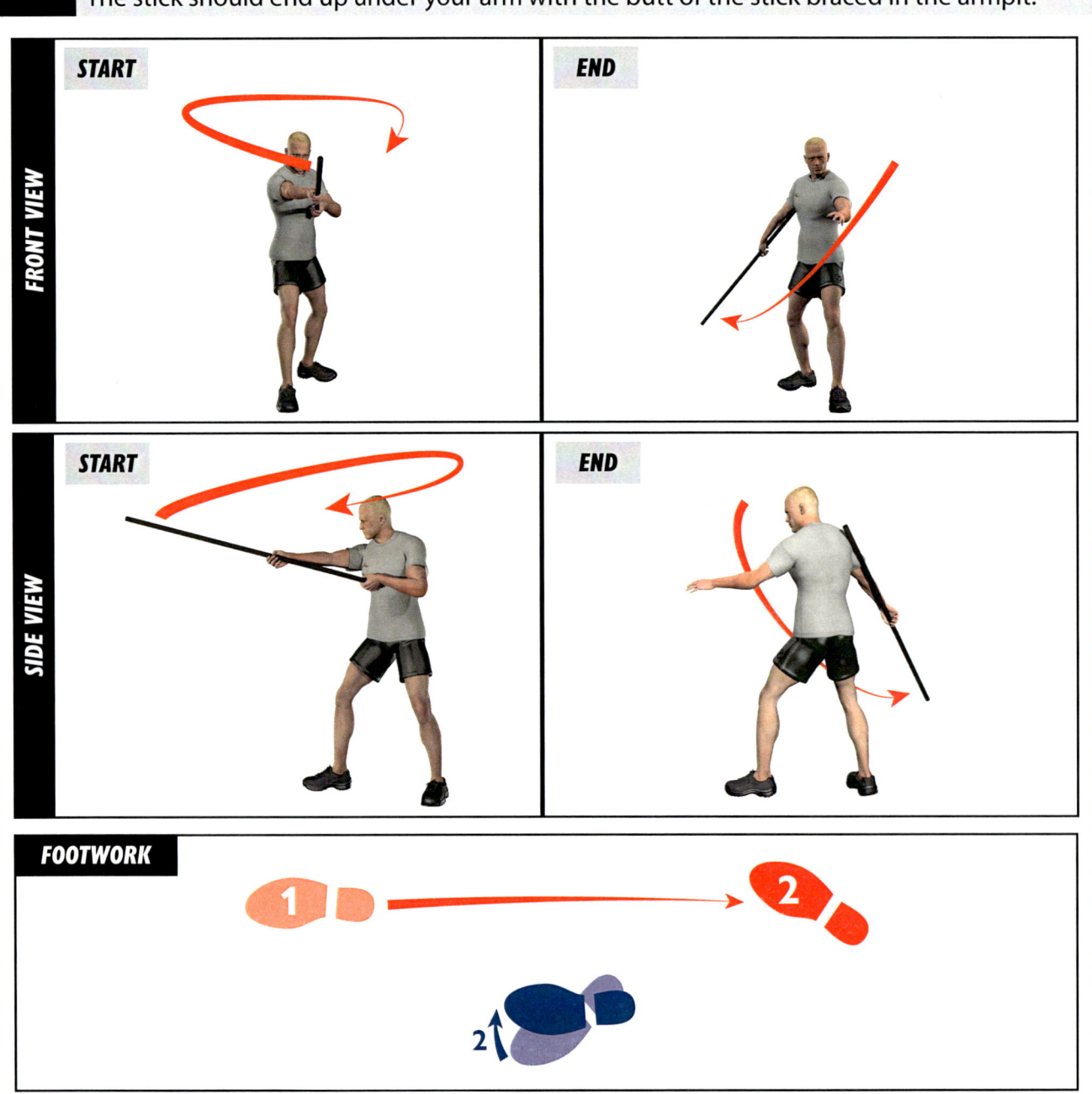

FRONT VIEW — START / END

SIDE VIEW — START / END

FOOTWORK

STICK TRAINING

Four-Direction Drill (4 of 8)

4 **DIAGONAL STRIKE:** Step forward with the right foot as you bring the stick back along the path it just came, swinging over the head in a clockwise motion and then striking downward and to the left at a 45-degree angle.

FRONT VIEW — START / END

SIDE VIEW — START / END

FOOTWORK

STICK TRAINING

Four-Direction Drill (5 of 8)

5 **180-DEGREE TURN AND STRIKE:** Bring the stick back along the path it just came, raising it up and to the right and swinging it over your head in a counterclockwise motion. As you do this you will step forward with the left leg while spinning 180-degrees to your right. Your right leg will swing around and step back as you strike downward and to the right with the stick at a 45-degree angle, bringing the stick under your arm.

TOP VIEW

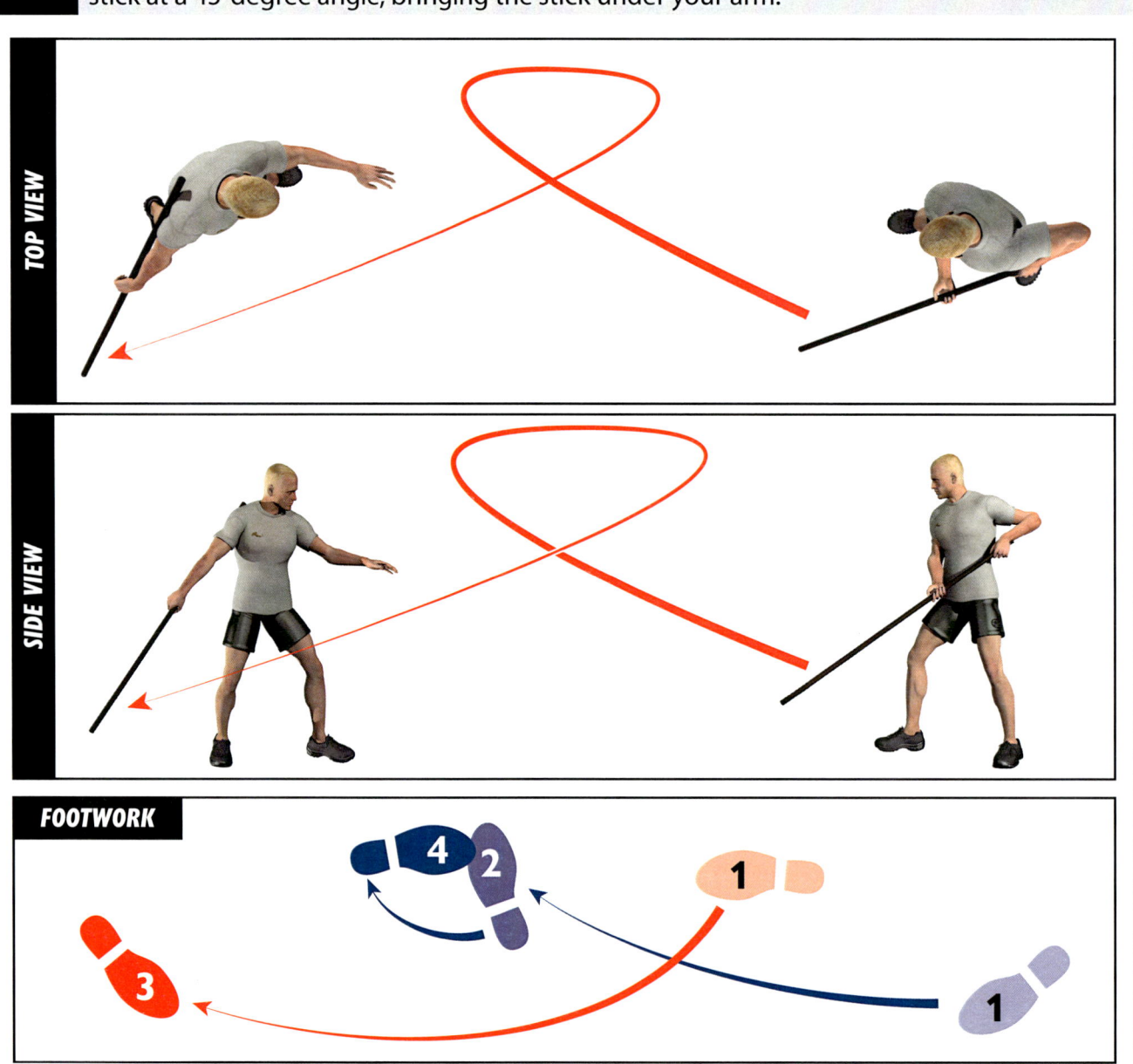

SIDE VIEW

FOOTWORK

STICK TRAINING

Four-Direction Drill (6 of 8)

6 **DIAGONAL STRIKE:** Step forward with the right foot as you bring the stick back along the path it just came, swinging over the head in a clockwise motion and then striking downward and to the left at a 45-degree angle.

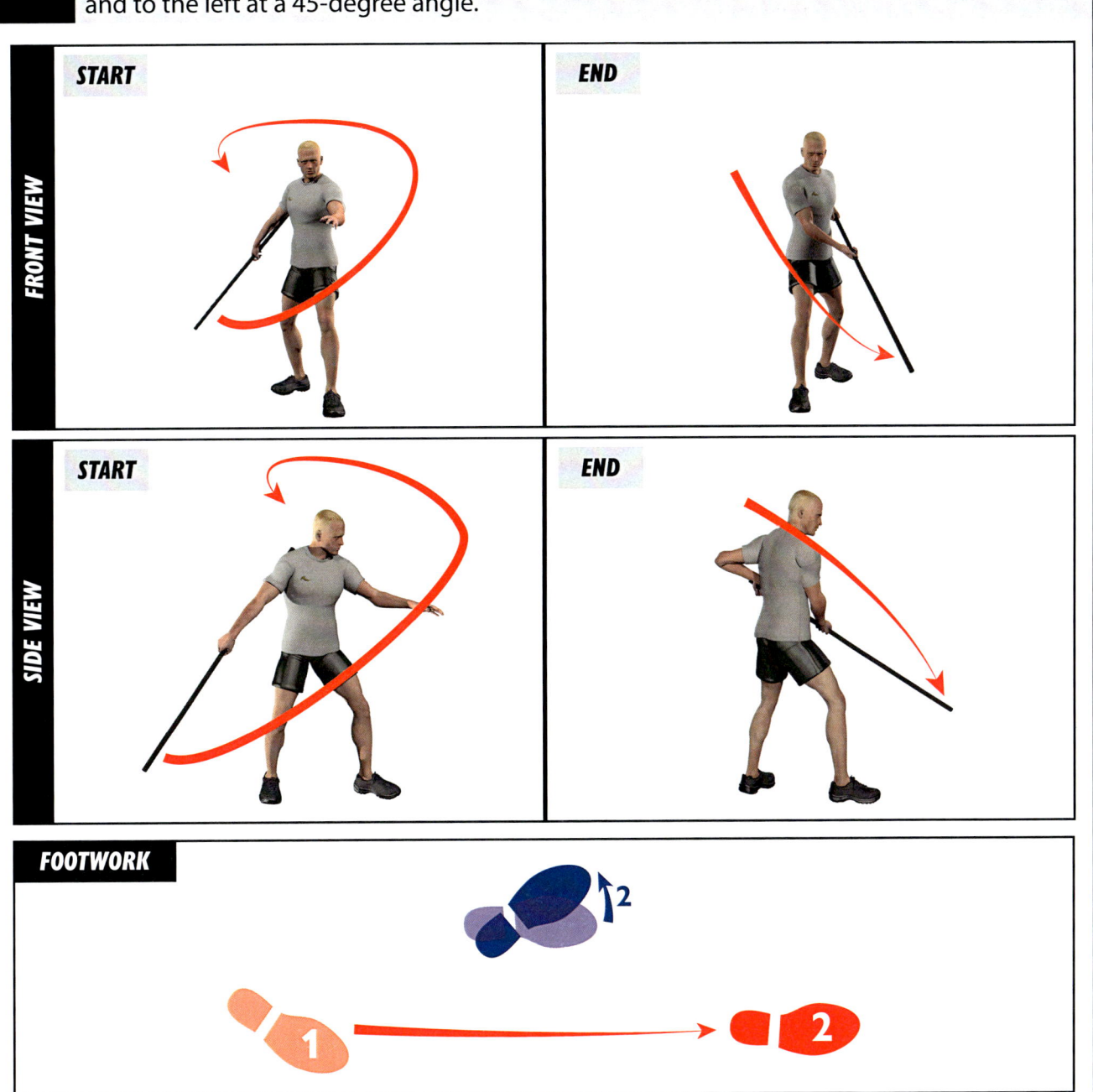

FRONT VIEW — START / END

SIDE VIEW — START / END

FOOTWORK

STICK TRAINING

Four-Direction Drill (7 of 8)

7 **180-DEGREE TURN AND STRIKE:** Bring the stick back along the path it just came, raising it up and to the right and swinging it over your head in a counterclockwise motion. As you do this you will step forward with the left leg while spinning 180-degrees to your right. Your right leg will swing around and step back as you strike downward and to the right with the stick at a 45-degree angle, bringing the stick under your arm.

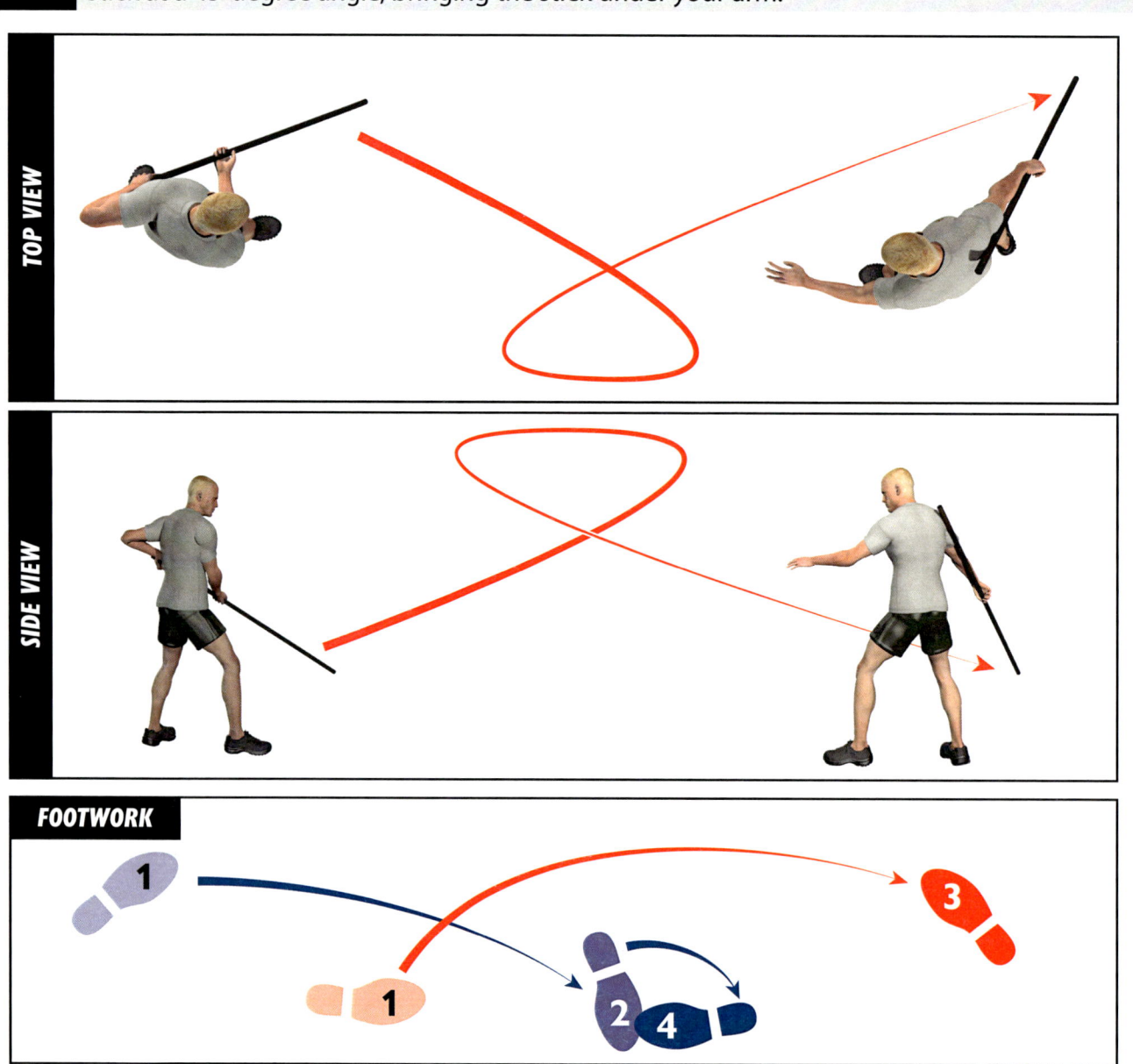

STICK TRAINING

Four-Direction Drill (8 of 8)

8 **90-DEGREE TURN AND STRIKE:** Bring the stick back along the path it just came, swinging over the head in a clockwise motion and then striking downward and to the left at a 45-degree angle. As you do this you will perform a 90-degree turn to your left by stepping forward and to the left with the right leg and then letting the left leg step back as you strike. At this point you can repeat the full 8-step sequence as many times as you would like.

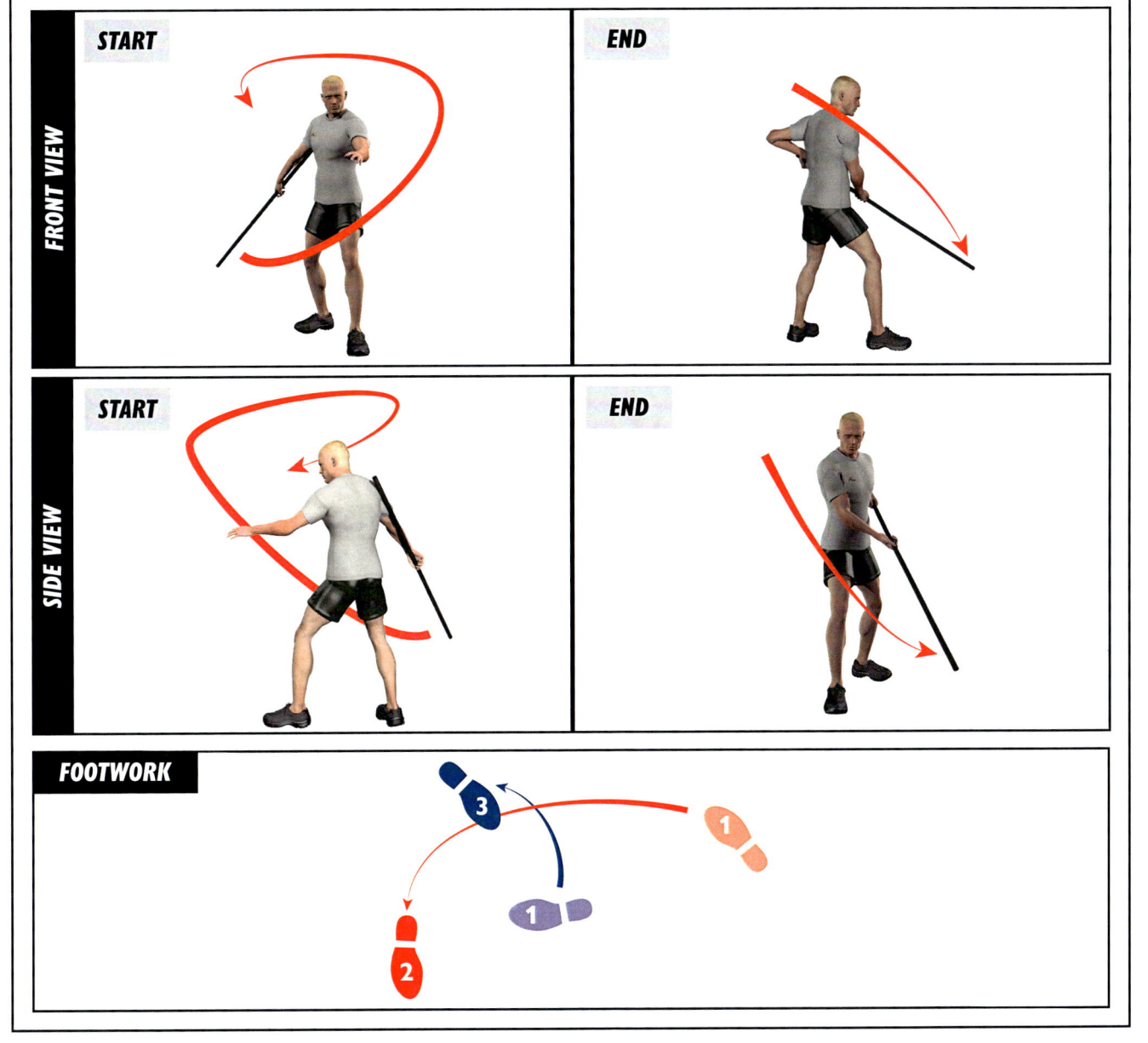

STICK TRAINING

Four-Direction Drill (Complete Sequence)

To further clarify the movement sequence, the diagram below shows the ending position for each of the 8 moves in sequence from the side and top. Once again, since the sequence ends with a 90-degree turn, if you repeat the full sequence four times you will rotate around in a full circle, ending the drill facing the same direction you started.

SIDE VIEW

TOP VIEW

SPORTS TRAINING

Benefits of Sports

Like martial arts and stick training, playing sports is one of the best ways to build several athletic skills and attributes simultaneously. All sports offer benefits for the combat athlete, however, depending on your operational requirements, some sports may prove more useful than others. Below are some sports that can be useful to the tactical athlete:

EXTREME/ADVENTURE OUTDOOR RACING: There are a growing number of sports in which competitors have to move over rough terrain and encounter a variety of obstacles or challenges along the way. These sports can be particularly useful for infantry and special operations personnel, or for units that have to operate in difficult terrain for long periods. The more realistic the race challenges are, the more useful the sport will be. Races that contain obstacle courses are particularly beneficial.

MARTIAL ARTS, WRESTLING AND BOXING: While fighting arts technically fall under the category of skills training, it is still possible to practice sport or recreational martial arts primarily for fitness purposes. In addition to the stick/weapons training already described, other common boxing, wrestling and martial arts exercises can be a great workout and will also help build your fighting ability. Striking or punching drills against a bag can be particularly effective when combined with endurance and speed intervals.

SQUASH AND RACQUETBALL: These sports are useful because they simultaneously build quickness, agility, hand-eye coordination and cardiovascular endurance. The quick lateral movement and rotation of the hips is similar to movements used in martial arts and close quarters battle.

ROUGH SPORTS (FOOTBALL, RUGBY ETC.): While rough sports are often not a good choice for units that want to avoid unnecessary injury, experiencing rough physical contact can greatly improve physical and psychological toughness. It can be difficult for some to develop the aggressive, fighter's mindset without experiencing real combat. Rough sports can in some ways replicate the experience of combat without risking death or serious injury. Such sports can also be useful to help instructors evaluate trainees for aggressiveness and courage.

SOCCER AND BASKETBALL: Soccer and basketball are useful because they offer a great workout without a high risk of injury. Both sports demand constant movement and quick change of direction. In addition, both sports build high levels of teamwork and cooperation. While soccer focuses mostly on lower body coordination, basketball focuses on agility and upper body coordination. Soccer is also a particularly useful sport for units that have to operate with or train foreign forces, since soccer is a very popular sport in the vast majority of countries around the world. Developing soccer skills might help a unit build rapport with foreign partners.

OTHER BALANCE AND COORDINATION DRILLS

Overview

In addition to martial arts training and sports, there are specialized drills that can be helpful in building balance, coordination and dexterity. When possible, it is helpful to combine these various drills and integrate them into mobility and strength workouts. This will allow the drills to provide some of the same advantages as stick training and sports training by challenging the body in multiple ways at one time. It is also helpful when drills relate to actual combat skills or attributes and replicate realistic combat conditions.

BALANCE BOARDS AND SLACKLINE: There are a number of training tools specifically designed to build balance. Balance boards vary in level of difficulty. Some only require stability in two directions while others require omnidirectional stability. Slacklines increase difficulty by incorporating an elastic bounce effect into the balance drill. Balance boards that incorporate inflatable balls provide a similar challenge. Once you master a balance drill you can increase difficulty by either standing on one foot, closing your eyes or both. As already stated, balance drills can prove more useful if you attempt to perform another physical activity while standing on the balance device.

BALL BOUNCE: Bouncing a ball off of a wall and catching it is a simple and useful way to build hand-eye coordination and dexterity. Using a very light ball, like a Ping-Pong ball can help develop greater finger dexterity while using a heavier ball can help build strength. To increase difficulty, you can bounce the ball off an uneven surface like a stone wall. This is particularly effective when using a Ping-Pong ball and will simultaneously build reaction-time, hand-eye coordination and dexterity.

MUSICAL INSTRUMENTS: Some musical instruments like the guitar or piano require very high levels of finger dexterity and coordination. Therefore, learning to play these instruments can be a fun and rewarding way to build up your hands and improve your ability to perform small-motor tactical activities like tying knots, bypassing locks, clearing weapon malfunctions or performing surgical procedures.

JUGGLING: Learning to juggle is a simple way to build hand-eye coordination. Interspersing juggling or other coordination drills between intense exercises like sprints or circuit training is also a good way to evaluate how exertion affects your dexterity and coordination.

TETHER BALL: Attaching a ball to a cord or rope and then tying the rope to a vertical pole or tree is an easy way to create an excellent coordination training tool. You can practice throwing, catching or hitting the ball at different angles as it spins around the tether. You can use balls of varying weights, shapes and sizes based on preference.

HAND AND GRIP TRAINING

Overview

Grip strength is one of the most important attributes for the tactical athlete but is also one of the most neglected areas of training. Grip is important for recoil management when shooting, for controlling adversaries in a physical encounter, for climbing, and for dragging or carrying heavy objects. If you perform upper-body strength training exercises, those exercises will generally help improve grip strength as well, but it is generally advisable to perform additional grip exercises. Building hand toughness is also important and therefore it is generally not optimal for the tactical athlete to wear protective gloves when lifting weights etc. Calluses will help protect your hands from injury in the field.

GRIP STRENGTHENER: Grip strengtheners are inexpensive, portable and easy to use. Generally, the best way to use the grip strengthener is to squeeze as tightly as you can and hold the squeeze for an extended interval, at least 10 seconds. In a tactical situation, you will most likely need to maintain a grip for an extended period. Therefore, squeezing and holding is generally better than a quick pumping motion. Also, the type of low resistance grip strengtheners available in most commercial stores are less effective than professional grip strengtheners with higher resistance.

GRIP MACHINES: Grip machines are another effective way to build grip strength and can be found in most gyms. They are not as portable as handheld grip strengtheners but they frequently allow for adjustable resistance. The principles for using the grip machine are the same as for using the grip strengthener.

LEDGE/BAR HANG OR SANDBAG CARRY: Using your hands under realistic conditions is another great way to build functional grip strength. Two examples are hanging from a ledge or bar for as long as possible, carrying sandbags or using sandbags instead of weights for performing strength exercises. There are countless possibilities of exercises that will build different types of strength.

EXERCISE & TRAINING TECHNIQUES
Flexibility, Recovery and Nutrition

For the most advanced combat athletes, flexibility, recovery and nutrition are actually the most important aspects of the fitness program. The reason for this is because less advanced or less experienced combat athletes primarily focus on trying to reach the level of maximum exertion without quitting or losing motivation. For the elite combat athlete, pushing oneself to the limit is not a goal or a challenge but the norm. Once you have learned to push yourself to the limit every day without quitting, the obstacle standing in the way of your progress is no longer your ability to push yourself harder but rather your ability to prevent your body from breaking.

The elite combat athlete pushes the limits every day. Working on flexibility, recovery and nutrition helps extend those limits, allowing the athlete to push harder and go farther without risking injury. Therefore, at the most advanced levels of combat fitness, the real test is the efficiency and effectiveness of your recovery systems. If you do a better job of recovering, you can take only one day's rest after a long ruck instead of needing two days. You can work out two or three times per day and still be ready for more the next morning.

You should keep your recovery routines as simple and streamlined as possible. The purpose of recovery must always be to help you achieve better and faster results with your fitness program. It is possible to get overly focused on recovery and waste valuable time that you could spend on training.

FLEXIBILITY

Dynamic Stretches (1 of 4)

Dynamic stretches involve performing functional movements that bring your limbs near to the limits of their range of motion. It is best to conduct dynamic stretches before a workout as part of your warmup routine. Dynamic stretches warm up and loosen the muscles, getting them used to stretching and contracting. Dynamic stretches also stimulate the release of synovial fluids in the joints which help reduce friction and prevent join pain and damage.

HIP SWING: Stand on one leg and swing the other leg forward and backward in a relaxed way, slowly increasing the range of motion with each sweep. If you have trouble maintaining your balance you can place your hand on a wall.

LATERAL HIP SWING: This is the same as the regular hip swing except you will swing your leg laterally (from side to side). To stabilize yourself you can place your hands on a wall in front of you.

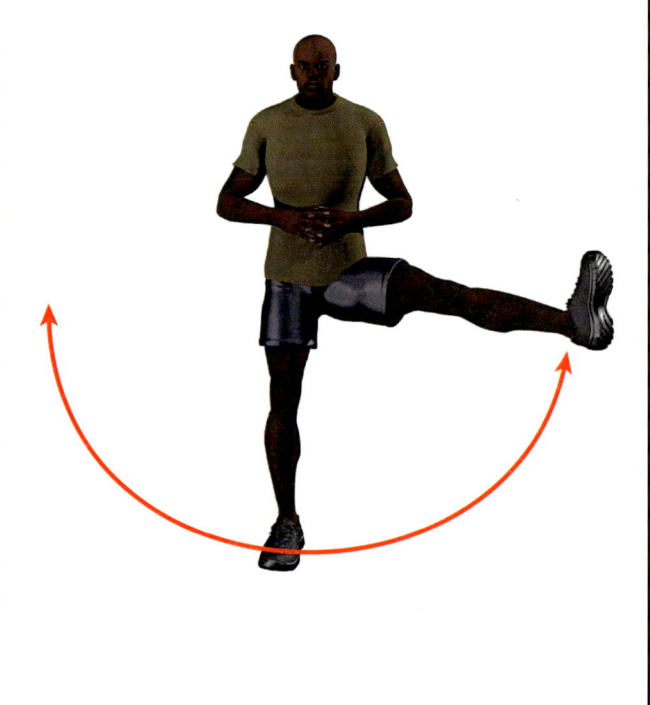

FLEXIBILITY

Dynamic Stretches (2 of 4)

LEG EXTENSION: Raise one knee at a 90-degree angle and then extend your lower leg forward until it is fully extended. Then return the lower leg to the starting position and repeat the movement at least 5 times.

HAMSTRING SQUEEZE: Stand tall with both feet together, then raise one leg rearward, bending at the knee, attempting to touch your heel to your buttocks. Return to the starting position and repeat the movement at least 5 times.

FLEXIBILITY

Dynamic Stretches (3 of 4)

KNEE CIRCLES: Stand with your feet and knees together, bend at the knees and waist and place your hands on your knees. Rotate your knees first clockwise and then counterclockwise.

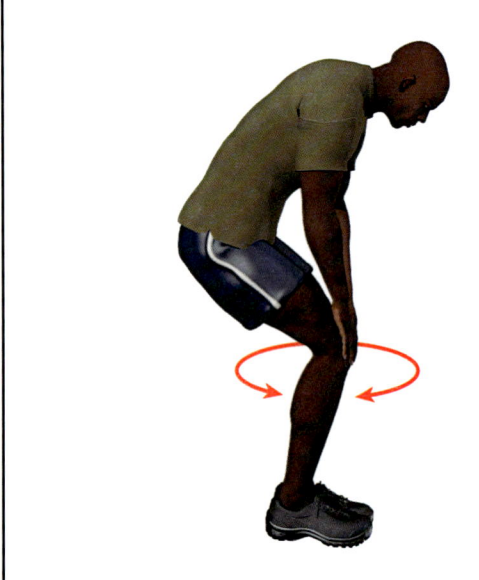

CALF EXTENSIONS: Stand tall with your feet shoulder-width apart. Push through the ground and stand up on your toes, raising your heels off the ground as high as possible. Then lower your heels and raise your toes off the ground as high as possible. Return to the starting position and repeat the full movement at least 5 times.

FLEXIBILITY

Dynamic Stretches (4 of 4)

SHOULDER CIRCLES: Relax the arms and rotate the shoulders slowly, forward and backward. You can also perform the same movement with your arms hanging at your sides, rolling only the shoulders backwards and forwards.

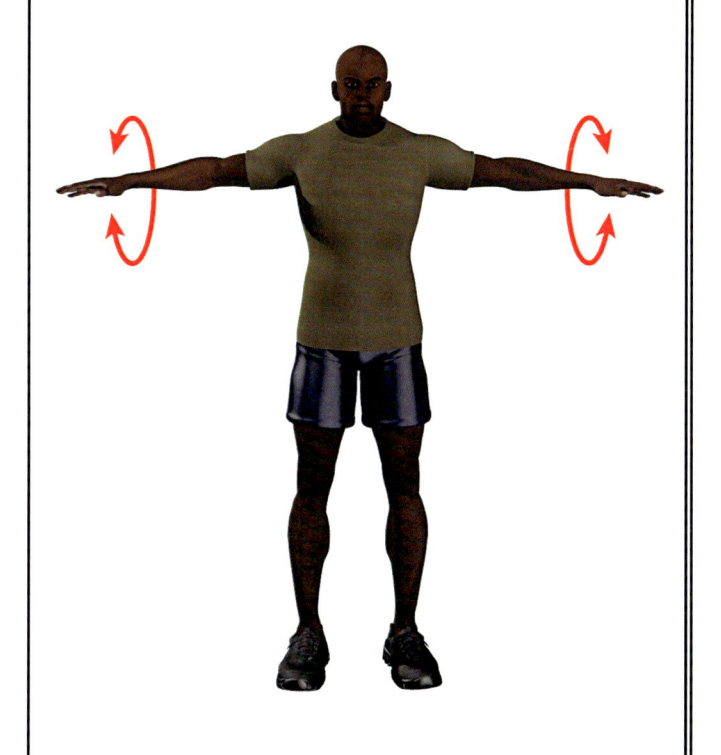

NECK CIRCLES: Let the shoulders drop into a relaxed position, then slowly rotate the head clockwise and counterclockwise.

FLEXIBILITY

Static Stretches (1 of 3)

Static stretches are designed to increase flexibility and lengthen the muscles. Having loose, flexible muscles improves muscle performance, shortens recovery time and reduces the chances of injury. It is best to perform static stretches after a workout, when the muscles are warm. When conducting static stretches, it is important not to bounce or strain too hard while stretching, since doing so can cause injury. There are a wide variety of static stretches, each with their own advantages and disadvantages. Below are a few examples of simple stretches that are both safe and effective.

GROIN STRETCH: Stand tall and spread your legs as far as possible with your feet on the ground and your toes pointed forwards. Once your legs as spread to a point of minor discomfort, hold that position, place your hands on your hips and move your hips forward, backward and rotate them left and right. When you feel comfortable, you can spread your legs further.

HAMSTRING STRETCH: Sit tall on a bench with one foot extended in front of you resting on the bench and the other foot flat on the ground. For some, just sitting upright (without letting the lower back sink or bend) will stretch the hamstring. Once you can sit upright, bend forward at the waist while keeping the back straight. At the same time, push through the heel while letting your toes flex back towards you. This will stretch the hamstring from both ends.

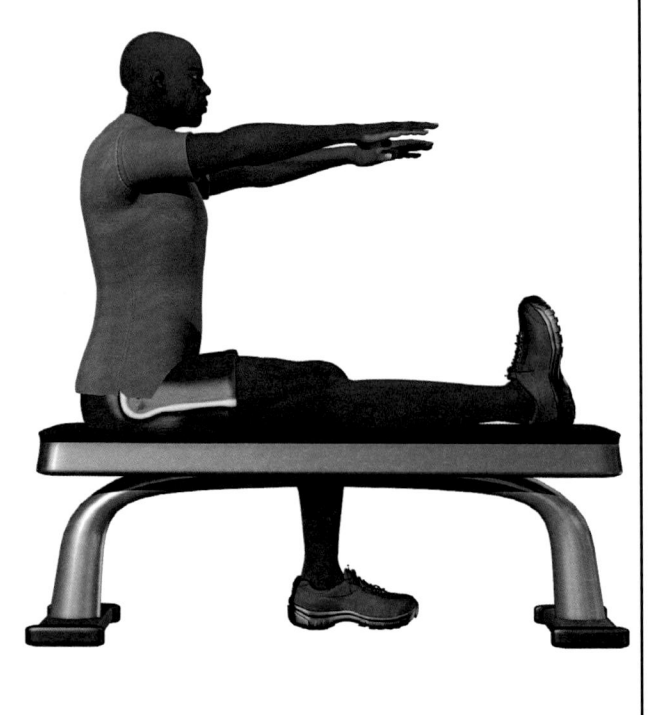

FLEXIBILITY

Static Stretches (2 of 3)

QUAD STRETCH: Stand upright and place one foot on a raised platform behind you. It may be necessary to use props, sandbags or similar objects to adjust the height of the platform. Bend the front knee slightly and drive the hips forward. You should feel a stretch in your quadriceps. You can intensify the stretch by raising the platform, bending your front knee or increasing your distance from the platform.

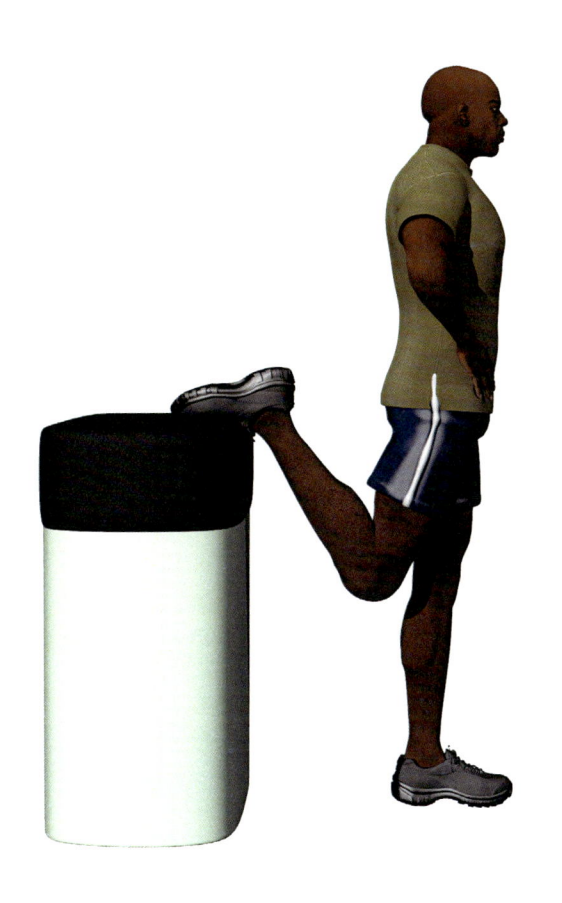

HIP STRETCH: Start in the lunge position with your rear knee on the ground and rear toe pointed. Keep your back straight and drive your hip forward. You should feel the stretch in your hip flexor.

FLEXIBILITY

Static Stretches (3 of 3)

GLUTE STRETCH: Stand facing a platform that is close to waist high. Lift your foot up and place it on the platform so that your lower leg is lying nearly flat in front of you. You may need to place an object under your knee if you are not flexible enough to let it lie on the platform. Bend forward at the waist while keeping the back straight to intensify the stretch.

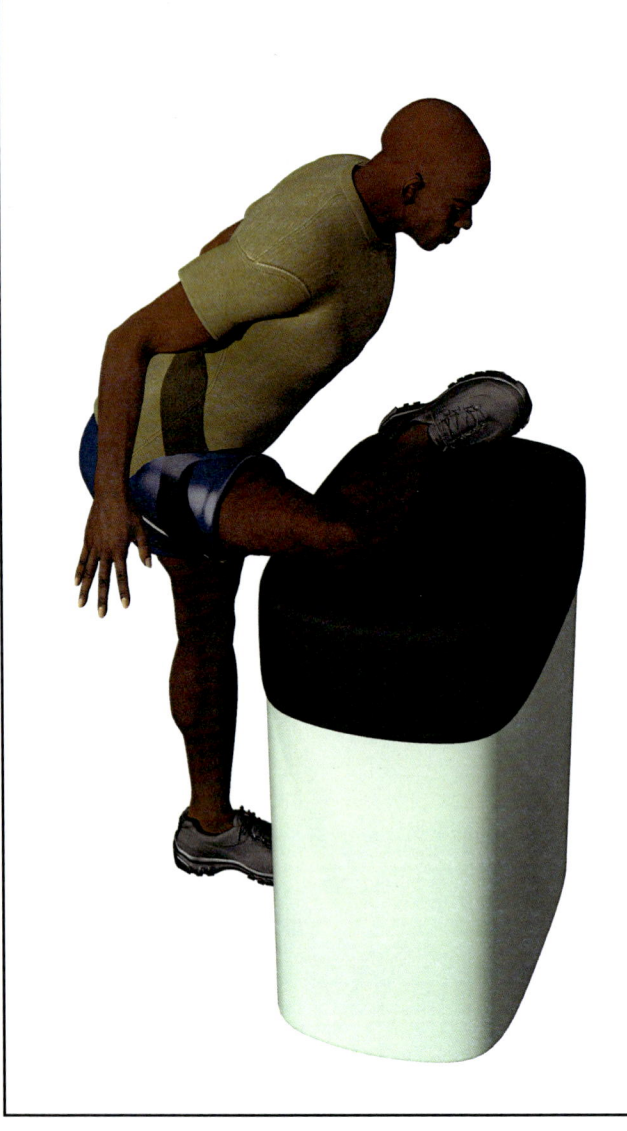

CALF STRETCH: One of the more effective calf stretches employs a calf wedge. Some calf wedges have adjustable levels of intensity. Stand tall on the wedge with one foot and let your weight sink through your heel. To intensify the stretch, you can lean forward or use a steeper wedge. If you do not have a calf wedge, you can use any solid object like a brick, stair or curb.

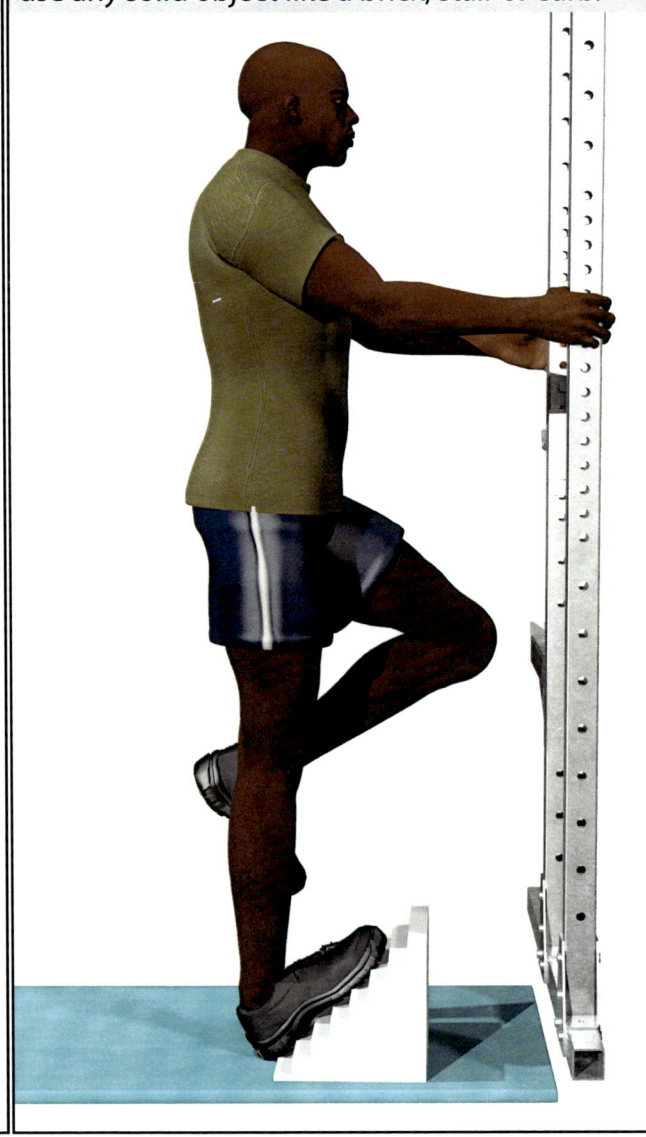

RECOVERY

Foam Roller and Massage

Massage, particularly deep tissue athletic massage is an outstanding tool for promoting recovery and keeping muscles healthy. Unfortunately, because most tactical athletes do not have the same schedule and budget as professional athletes, frequent massage sessions are impractical. However, there are a number of massage tools that are cheap, effective and easy to use. When using these tools, you should focus on muscles that are tight or appear to have painful "knots" in them. These knots (also known as myofascial trigger points) are spots of tense, irritable muscle fibers. When applying pressure with the various massage tools described below, it is best to focus on these trigger points in an effort to "release" them. When you press on a trigger point it will be painful, however, after continued massaging and pressure, the trigger point will release and will no longer be painful. Releasing trigger points improves muscle health, performance and flexibility while speeding recovery.

FOAM ROLLER: The foam roller is one of the cheapest and most effective myofascial release and massage tools. There is no fixed formula for how to use the foam roller. Once of the most common techniques is to place the roller on the ground and lie on it sideways so the roller can roll up and down the side of your leg. There are frequently numerous trigger points along the side of the leg. You can experiment with rolling quickly or slowly, stopping to sink into trigger points when you find them. This can be very painful at first but will grow easier with practice. You can use similar techniques to massage the front and back of the legs, calves and lower back. You can also place the roller on the wall to target the arms and upper back. You can also experiment using rollers of different sizes, shapes and hardness.

BALL ROLLER: It can be easier to target some muscles using a small ball instead of a roller. Balls made of hard material like lacrosse balls can be particularly effective. Place the ball on the ground or on the wall, then lean your weight into it, shifting the body to allow the ball to press against painful trigger points until they are released. The ball roller is particularly useful for trigger points in the upper back around the edges of the scapula (shoulder blades).

HAND ROLLER: Another useful tool is a hand roller. You can purchase purpose-built hand rollers from athletic or running stores but you can also use improvised rollers like a rolling-pin or wooden dowel. Holding the roller in both hands will give you a better angle to target certain muscles.

RECOVERY

Ice, Heat and Topical Analgesic (1 of 2)

Ice and heat therapy are two of the oldest and most effective recovery methods. Heat is useful for soothing sore muscles and treating cramps or muscle tightness. By increasing blood flow to the muscles, heat can help muscles recover faster and reduce soreness after workouts. Heat is particularly useful when applied before, during or after massage type therapy. Ice is a better option if you are experiencing sore joints, tendons or any other kind of inflammation. Ice will reduce inflammation but will also have positive effects similar to those of heat therapy, since blood will rush into the muscles as they warm up after the ice exposure. Using ice and heat therapy after every workout will greatly reduce your recovery time and lower your chances of injury. Topical analgesic is an ointment or cream that you can apply directly to the muscles that will have similar effects to heat or ice.

LOWER-BODY ICE BATH: The ice bath is one of the most effective ice therapy techniques. Fill a bathtub with six bags of ice (approximately 10 lbs. each) and fill the remainder of the bath with water. When you sit in the tub the ice should cover your legs completely but should not come above your hip bones. DO NOT submerge your upper body in the ice due to risk of heart attack. It can also be useful to cover your toes with socks or neoprene toe warmers to prevent injury. Sit in the ice for 15-20 minutes. Follow the ice bath with a hot shower. Note that some people may experience uncontrollable trembling during or after the ice bath. If this occurs, stop the ice bath and remain in a hot shower until the trembling stops.

ICE PACKS: Ice packs allow you to focus your cold therapy on a specific joint or muscle that is sore. When applying the ice pack, it is best to apply it directly to the skin to achieve the coldest temperature. Apply the ice pack to each location for 15-20 minutes.

ICE CUBE/CUP: You can use a single ice cube (or paper cup filled with ice) to rub ice on a sore bone or joint. This technique is particularly effective for dealing with shin splints.

HOT BATH/WHIRLPOOL: Sitting in a hot bath or whirlpool is a great way to relax muscles and reduce soreness after a workout. It can be useful to perform mild stretches while in the hot water and adding Epsom Salt to the water can provide added therapeutic effects.

HEATING PAD: Heating pads come in a variety of forms and can be used in a similar way as the ice pack. You can place the heating pad on sore muscles to increase blood flow and speed recovery.

SAUNA/STEAM ROOM: Sitting in the sauna or steam room after workouts will aid your recovery and has numerous other health benefits. Steam rooms will also help clear your nasal passages. It can be useful to perform stretches while in the sauna or steam room, since the muscles will be warm and pliable. Remain in the heat for at least 15-minutes to achieve the desired effects.

RECOVERY

Ice, Heat and Topical Analgesic (2 of 2)

CONTRAST SHOWER: The contrast shower has numerous health benefits and is also good for building discipline and resistance to cold. Begin by standing in the shower and slowly increasing the temperature until it is as hot as you can bear without damaging the skin. Let the hot water flow over your entire body including your head and face and remain under the water for at least ten seconds. Then, turn the hot water off completely and switch to all cold water. Wait for the water to turn cold and stand under it, letting it flow over your whole body. You may need to adjust position to ensure the cold covers your entire body. Once you begin to feel the cold numb your body or the cold grows difficult to bear, switch back to the same hot temperature you started with. It can be useful to mark the point on the faucet that delivers the desired heat to avoid burning yourself. Transition in this way between heat and cold at least four times. Always end the contrast shower with cold water. After incorporating the contrast shower into your daily routine, you will feel its positive effects immediately.

TOPICAL ANALGESIC: Topical analgesic is one of the easiest recovery tools to use since all you have to do is rub the ointment or cream on your muscles. Once again, it is useful to apply the analgesic to muscles that are particularly sore or contain painful trigger points. It is best to apply the analgesic after a workout and it is also possible to use topical analgesic in combination with foam roller or massage therapy.

RECOVERY

Sleep, Rest and Meditation

Sleep is one of the most essential and powerful tools for recovery. A tactical athlete who gets adequate sleep will achieve much quicker results than an athlete who is sleep deprived. Ideally, you should strive to sleep 6-8 hours each day to achieve peak mental and physical performance. However, the nature of the tactical profession can make this goal completely unrealistic. Depending on operational requirements, it may be impossible to get even four hours of sleep per night for an extended period of time. The important point is to realize that less sleep will likely degrade your performance so you should strive to get as much sleep as possible. However, there are techniques that can help you get better rest and recovery, whether or not you are able to get 6-8 hours of sleep.

POWER NAP: While naps might not seem compatible with the lifestyle of many tactical athletes, they can greatly improve your performance. If possible, try to take your nap roughly in the middle of your waking cycle or during your lunch break. The diet suggestions provided later in this book can help you free up your lunch break for naps or other training. It is important to keep your nap less than one-hour or it may throw off your natural sleep rhythm. Naps are particularly useful when you are learning new physical skills or movements. Your brain will only develop "motor programs" for new movements when you are sleeping. Therefore, adding an additional sleep period to your day will allow you to learn new skills and movements much faster.

MINDFUL BREATHING: One of the most simple and effective meditation and relaxation techniques simply involves being aware of your breathing. Your mind will naturally want to wander but the drill is to focus all your attention on your breathing for a short period (5-15 minutes). When focusing on your breathing, close your eyes and relax your body as much as possible. Focus on breathing slightly slower and deeper than normal. Performing this drill outside while listening to the sounds of nature can increase the level of relaxation for some people. If you have religious beliefs, you may want to incorporate prayer into the exercise. Performing even a short meditation session can improve your performance, reduce stress and speed recovery.

OTHER RELAXATION TOOLS AND TECHNOLOGY: There are numerous tools available to help you achieve better relaxation, awareness, mental and physical performance. These tools include biofeedback machines, heart rate variability monitors and sensory deprivation tanks. While these tools can be expensive, they are available to many military units and can be found in some physical therapy centers and hospitals. If you can access such tools they may prove very helpful for training and recovery.

NUTRITION

Performance Diet Principles

The optimal diet or nutrition program may vary dramatically depending on your unique physical characteristics, personal preferences and specific mission requirements. Selecting and designing your optimal diet is a highly personal process and there are no fixed rules to follow. Once you have developed good tactical and physical performance evaluations, the best option is to test different diets and see which one offers the best results. If a diet seems to be working for you, it is wise to stick with it but always look for ways to modify it and improve it over time. Below is an example of one approach to performance nutrition for tactical athletes and some suggestions for developing a nutrition program.

FOOD GROUPS AND NUTRIENT INTAKE: The tactical athlete should eat as many healthy foods as possible and try to consume at least the recommended daily value for each of the six USDA food groups: grains, fruits, vegetables, meats, dairy and fats. However, the amount of each nutrient consumed might vary from USDA recommendations. Natural, unprocessed, whole foods are generally the healthiest options. Essentially, if you are training as hard as you can and pushing yourself to the limit, you should not limit your food intake but should rather eat as much as possible. The key is eating healthy foods. If operational requirements bring your level of exertion down and you start gaining weight, you should reduce your nutrient intake accordingly.

HIGH-PROTEIN, HIGH-CARB, LOW-FAT: When you are training at the highest possible intensity level, it can be helpful to maintain maximum protein and carbohydrate intake in order to sustain your energy level, support recovery and prevent your body from breaking down. Protein (especially red meat protein) provides the building blocks for muscle growth while carbohydrates (especially complex carbohydrates like whole grains) provide the most efficient and lasting fuel for your muscles. By minimizing the fat in your diet, you will be able to stay lean while giving your body plenty of fuel for maximum exertion. A low-fat diet will also streamline your digestion, allowing you to absorb nutrients faster and fuel your muscles more quickly.

SMALL MEALS: When possible, it is better to eat multiple small meals throughout the day than it is to eat large meals. Eating small meals will help you maintain a steady blood-sugar level and avoid overtaxing your digestive system at any given time. This will result in increased and more consistent energy levels throughout the day.

EFFICIENCY AND PRACTICALITY: One of the biggest reasons tactical athletes develop unhealthy nutrition habits is simply because their operational requirements are so demanding that they do not have time to shop for or prepare the healthiest meals. Therefore, the ideal performance diet also has to be simple and practical to meet your highly demanding tactical lifestyle. If it is not, you will likely have no choice but to break from your diet and eat whatever is available when you have the chance.

NUTRITION

Performance Diet Example (1 of 2)

The principles above can be difficult to put into practice, especially considering how busy the life of a tactical professional can be. Below is an example diet plan that follows all the principles above in an efficient way and will provide the tactical athlete with very high levels of energy for intense training regimens. Once again, this is only one suggestion for a nutrition program and the optimal program for you might look much different.

SHOPPING AND FOOD PREPARATION: Having to constantly shop for food or go out to restaurants will waste valuable training time and personal time. It is optimal to purchase and prepare an entire week of meals in a single day, then store them in the refrigerator or freezer for quick consumption. With practice, you will be able to purchase and prepare all your meals for the week in just a few hours or less.

LUNCH-BREAKFAST FLIP: You will need a high intake of protein and carbs to sustain your intensity level. If you conduct your main workout first thing in the morning it is best to have a high-protein, high-carb meal following your morning workout focusing on the meat and grain food groups. Therefore, you will essentially eat "lunch for breakfast." Good breakfast selections may include hearty portions of chicken, fish, rice or potatoes with no additional fat or sugar intake. By eating a big meal immediately after your first workout, you will be pumping plenty of nutrients into your thirsty muscles to repair them and energize them for the day.

"NO-LUNCH" CONCEPT: Having already consumed roughly half of your daily meat and grain intake for breakfast, you can spread out your intake of fruits and vegetables throughout the day. This takes the "small-meals" concept to the next level. You will essentially eliminate lunch altogether and consume a constant flow of nutrients all day long until it is time for your afternoon-evening workout. One efficient way to do this is to blend a wide variety of fruits and vegetables into smoothies and sip them throughout the day. In the end, you will end up consuming or exceeding your daily value of fruits and vegetables every day, which can be very difficult to accomplish using the traditional three-meal model. In addition, blending your fruits and vegetables will help you absorb more nutrients and digest them faster.

NUTRITION

Performance Diet Example (2 of 2)

BENEFITS OF "NO-LUNCH": By eliminating lunch and instead consuming nutrients throughout the day, you will not need to take a "lunch break." This will allow you to use lunch time for an additional workout, range time, skill training or a power nap. Consuming nutrients throughout the day will also keep your stomach relatively empty, allowing you to workout and train constantly without cramping if needed. Smoothies and drinks are also easy to carry, providing you with a ready source of nutrition and energy that you can take with you anywhere, whether you are on the range, on the road or in a briefing.

HIGH PROTEIN AND CARB DINNER: You will eat dinner after your second workout, focusing on meats and grains as you did for breakfast. For dinner, large portions of red meats like beef and lamb are a good choice since red meats provide the full spectrum of amino acids needed for muscle growth. Healthy complex carbs like rice, potatoes or wheat will provide a good complement to the meat. Once again, it is best not to add any additional fat or sugar to your meal.

NUTRITION

Supplements

When used correctly and in moderation, supplements can help you achieve a significant increase in your performance. There are many different philosophies about supplements and you should choose the approach that works for you and fits your operational requirements. In general terms, it is important to remember that it is not ideal to become dependent on supplements if there is a chance they will be unavailable in the combat environment. It is also generally safest to use supplements that are as natural as possible and that have the fewest number of potential side-effects. Below are some principles and suggestions for using supplements:

VITAMINS AND PILLS: It can be useful to take daily vitamins and other natural supplements in pill form, particularly if you are unable to get all of your required vitamins through your daily food intake. Some useful vitamins and pill supplements include multi-vitamins, vitamin-C, fish oil and garlic extract.

CAFFEINE: Studies show that consuming caffeine before a workout can improve workout intensity and performance. There are a wide variety of caffeine athletic supplements including shots, gels and candies specifically designed for this purpose.

CARB SUPPLEMENTS: Consuming carbs before a workout can help you sustain your energy level throughout the workout. For particularly long workouts it can help to begin "carbo-loading" well before the workout begins. When conducting workouts longer than one hour, it can be helpful to consume a small carb supplement every hour to sustain energy. Once again, there are a wide selection of carb supplements including drinks and mixing powders designed for just this purpose.

PROTEIN SUPPLEMENTS: Studies have shown that consuming protein immediately after a workout can help accelerate muscle growth. Milk is a cheap and simple source of protein that is easy to consume after a workout. If you are unable to get enough protein through your normal diet you can use other natural protein supplements to boost your protein intake.

NUTRITION

Example Cooking/Preparation Instructions

The following are some general instructions for preparing meals for the performance diet program outlined on pages 112-113. These meals are only examples. You can use an unlimited combination of different ingredients or foods to create meals with similar nutritional benefits.

BREAKFAST: 1/2 pound of ground turkey cooked in chicken broth served in a soup with rice, bulger what or potatoes. Alternate every-other-day with broiled salmon served with rice, bulger what or potatoes. Roast chicken is another good meat alternative.

ALL DAY SMOOTHIE: Cook a combination of sweet potato, beets, carrots and broccoli in a pressure cooker, steamer or microwave. Place the cooked vegitables in a blender with berries (blueberries, rasberries, blackberries or strawberries etc.), raw tomatoes and raw greens (spinach, kale etc.). Mix in any protein, nutritional or phytonutrient powders and blend in the blender with water, coconut water or juice.

DINNER: 1 pound of ground beef or lamb cooked in chicken broth served in a soup with rice, bulger what or potatoes. An alternative is to cook a large beef or lamb roast and cut 1-pound servings each day. Cooking a beef or lamb stew is another alternative.

SECTION 2

PROGRAM DESIGN & TRACKING

PROGRAM DESIGN AND TRACKING
Workout and Fitness Program Design

While the previous section provided examples of exercises and fitness activities, this section explains how to tie those various sub-components together into a program that meets your operational needs. Probably the most important point to remember when designing a fitness program is that the design process never ends. The first version of your fitness program may not be ideal but it will provide a foundation for future designs and improvements. Therefore, it is not necessary to spend too much time designing your program at first. In many cases, you will just continue using your existing program, possibly with a few minor modifications. Then, as you track your progress and learn how to make the most of your combat performance evaluations, you can modify the program over time.

It would be impossible to discuss all the potential fitness program design options. This section only provides a general outline of some key design fundamentals such as scheduling, periodization and integration of different workout types. The second half of this section then provides an example of one approach to program design developed and refined by the Special Tactics Staff. We are not suggesting this approach is better than any other approach and it may not be the best fit for your requirements. However, it was necessary to use an example to show how the design concepts translate into reality.

Conversely, the Special Tactics approach does have many benefits. While it might not be the right fit for some tactical athletes, others may decide to incorporate elements of the Special Tactics approach into their workouts, or use the example program design as a baseline or template for designing a unit-level fitness program. Either way, we highly recommend that even if you do incorporate elements of the example workouts in the following sections, that you modify them as needed based on your personal/unit needs and preferences.

Finally, while much of the wording in this book refers to unit-level combat fitness programs, the exact same concepts can be applied at the individual level with minor modifications. An individual seeking to improve his/her combat fitness can design combat performance evaluations, record results and use those results to develop a personal combat fitness program. Civilians who are not military, law-enforcement or security personnel can still benefit from choosing a combat fitness program over another commercial program, since a combat fitness program will help improve their ability to survive in a crisis while protecting themselves and their families.

Workout Scheduling: Workout Time Blocks

One of the most critical factors that will drive workout planning is the time available for scheduling workouts. Ideally, the tactical athlete should work out every day with one "off-day" per week for recovery. Below are several examples of different time blocks for workouts and how to use them:

Morning Workout: This is one of the most common workouts. Units typically schedule approximately one-hour each morning before work begins for fitness training. Another common practice is to show up earlier on one day per week for an extended workout (like a long distance ruck, swim or tactical fitness session) that is 2-3 hours long.

Lunch Workout: Motivated individuals or units might choose to supplement their morning workout by training during lunch-break. Using the "no lunch" diet concept described earlier can make this easier to accomplish while not compromising nutrition.

Afternoon/Evening Workout: Working out immediately after the work or training day is another effective training option. Energy levels are typically higher in the afternoon when the body has had time to digest nutrients from breakfast and lunch. In addition, working out in the afternoon can be more efficient in terms of scheduling. If units work out in the morning, personnel will need time to shower and eat breakfast before the workday. If units work out after the work day, they will have more total work and training hours because they eliminate the breakfast/shower break.

Night Workout: Many units conduct most of their operations at night but spend relatively little time training in hours of darkness. Depending on what time the sun rises, it is possible to conduct night workouts in the early hours of the morning. It may also be useful to conduct extended workouts late at night. Such workouts might include long-range cross country movement at night or negotiating obstacles at night. If a unit has night vision devices, they should conduct physical training wearing these devices periodically to practice using them under physical exertion.

Short Workout: When used correctly, short workout sessions can prove to be some of the most effective sessions. While conventional wisdom suggests that a workout needs to be approximately one hour, it is possible to accomplish a great deal in only 15-minutes with a high-intensity workout. 15-minutes is a good target time for a short workout. In addition, it is usually possible to take a 15-minute break at multiple points throughout the day which makes it easy to squeeze multiple workouts into a tight schedule. Units that conduct one 15-minute workout in the morning, one 15-minute workout at lunch and one 15-minute workout after work can sometimes achieve better results than units that employ traditional one-hour workout schedules.

Workout Scheduling: Weekly Routines

Given the possible workout time blocks listed above, the next step is to schedule workouts throughout the week. To do this, you must schedule time blocks for workouts and then determine what sort of workout you will conduct in each time block. Below are some techniques for planning weekly routines.

Alternate Workout Types: It is generally best not to conduct the same type of workout two days in a row. For example, if you conduct a long distance run on Monday, it is better not to run the following day and instead focus on strength training or swimming etc. Alternating workouts in this manner will help your muscles recover faster and minimize the chances of injury.

Alternate Muscle Groups: If you choose to conduct strength training multiple days in a row, it may be good to alternate between different muscle groups. For example, you could conduct a lower body workout on Monday but then conduct an upper body workout on Tuesday while your lower body recovers. This also applies to different types of workouts that focus on the same muscle group. For example, if you conduct a lower body workout on Monday, it might not be effective to conduct a very intense hill-sprint workout on Tuesday.

Alternate Heavy and Light Days: In some cases, it may be useful to alternate heavy and light days. This can be particularly useful if you have other training or work obligations. Your light workout days can offer you time to focus on your other obligations. Light days can also help you recover and reduce the chances of injury.

Days Off: It is generally useful to take at least one day off per week and focus on getting maximum rest and recovery.

Number/ Length of Workouts: Based on your fitness goals and where you are in your training cycle/progress (see the next section of periodization), you can vary the volume of training you conduct each day or week. At one end of the spectrum, you might conduct two or three workouts per day or conduct long workouts that last for many hours. On the other end of the spectrum, you might conduct only a short workout each day, or even every other day, or even conduct a single workout per week. The volume of training you conduct in a given week will depend on the bigger picture of your periodization routine.

Workout Scheduling: Periodization

The concept of periodization comes from the athletic community and its intention is to help an athlete achieve his/her maximum performance or "peak" at the most important part of the athletic season. Because athletes have relatively fixed schedules for competition, they can go into a very high level of detail planning workout cycles to maximize performance at the critical time. Most tactical athletes have schedules that are much less predictable. You may not know when you will need to be at your best, particularly if you serve in a unit that must be ready to respond to an unexpected crisis with minimal warning. That being said, it is still useful to understand the concept of periodization in a general way, since alternating between a higher volume of training and a lower volume of training can prevent injury and increase progress over time.

Deployment Cycles: Some units have relatively predictable deployment cycles which offer the opportunity of more calculated periodization. These units might choose to take a few weeks of recovery when returning from deployment, with minimal training or no training. If the interval between deployments is short, the unit might choose to time the buildup in training volume to peak for the next deployment. If the interval between deployments is longer, the unit might want to go through two or more shorter cycles, building up to peak during key intermediate training events or exercises. There is no fixed formula for this but it is useful to vary the volume of training over time, cycling between higher and lower volume.

Improvised Cycles: If you serve in a unit without predictable deployment schedules, it can still be useful to vary the volume and intensity of your workouts over time. However, the variance will not be as dramatic and may have to be figured out on-the-fly based on your own intuition and performance feedback. If you start to feel fatigued or your body starts to break down, you may choose to reduce the volume of your training or take a few days off. Conversely, if you feel motivated, energized and are making faster progress than usual, you may want to increase the intensity level to capitalize on the momentum.

Operationally Dictated Cycles: In other cases, the nature and demands on your work will determine how much time and energy you have for physical training in a given period. In these cases, it is best to go with the flow and take advantage of the changes in your work conditions or schedule to achieve a degree of periodization in your training. For example, if you are assigned to conduct surveillance work for a few weeks and will have little time for workouts, take that time to rest the body and conduct light calisthenics or stretching to maintain your fitness. Alternatively, if you are sent on a trip to a mountainous area, you may decide to train more often to take advantage of the benefits of altitude training. Essentially, your work schedule and operational tempo may dictate your training cycles for you. Even if the cycles are not ideal, it is best not to resist them but rather attempt to make the most of them.

Fitness Program Design: Integrating Different Types of Workouts

Once you have determined the constraints of your workout schedule, you can go on to design your fitness program based on operational requirements. As already explained, the starting point for identifying operational requirements and setting fitness priorities in light of those requirements is the combat performance evaluation. Deficiencies that reveal themselves in the combat performance evaluation become the focus point for your fitness program. However, it is also possible to reach the same conclusions using logical thinking or group discussion. For example, it does not require numerous evaluations and experiments to determine that a maritime rescue unit should focus on swimming or that a long-range reconnaissance unit should prioritize cross-country movement. Therefore, through a combination of logic, discussion and evaluation, the first step is to identify the areas of focus for your fitness program. Depending on your focus, you will schedule the following types of workouts (or other types of your own design) into the available time blocks.

Traditional Running Workouts: These workouts are simple to conduct and provide numerous benefits for the tactical athletes. It is generally best not to conduct running workouts two days in a row. Running on Monday, Wednesday and Friday is a common weekly running routine. It also makes sense to conduct three different types of running workouts each week. For example: tempo run on Monday, interval run on Wednesday and distance run on Friday. It is generally wise to conduct a dynamic stretching routine before a run and a static stretching routine after the run. It can also be useful to conduct running drills or agility drills prior to a running workout as a warmup.

Traditional Strength Training Workouts: Traditional strength training workouts typically involve conducting roughly five strength training exercises with each exercise consisting of 3-5 sets with 4-12 repetitions per set and several minutes of rest between each set. Conducting 6 or fewer repetitions with heavier weight will build strength while conducting 12+ repetitions with lighter weight will improve endurance. It is important to remember that intense strength training with heavy weight increases the chances of injury.

Therefore, unless brute strength is critical for your operational requirements, it is often best to conduct strength training every-other-day or every 2-3 days, using lighter weight but conducting more repetitions.

Circuit Training: Circuit training involves conducting a combination of strength exercises with little or no rest between each set. It is also possible to incorporate plyometric and sprinting exercises into a circuit routine. Because you will take little or no rest between each set, circuit training helps you develop muscular and cardiovascular endurance while still building strength. A circuit will typically consist of 4-6 exercises that you will rotate through one after another. Once you finish one circuit you can rotate through the sequence again as many times as needed. Taking rest between circuits will help you push harder and faster in each circuit while taking no rest will build more endurance.

Speed Workouts: Because running speed is generally important for most tactical units, you may want to conduct dedicated speed workouts. Speed workouts must be kept relatively short (generally 15 minutes or less) because once you start to fatigue, you will no longer be able to push the limits of your speed. You can only build speed effectively when your muscles are moving at their maximum speed limit. Once you start to slow down due to fatigue, you are no longer building speed but are instead building strength and endurance. You can build speed by running short distance sprints or hill sprints of 200m or less. You should generally run between 4-6 sprints with full recovery between each sprint. Because sprinting workouts are taxing on the body and high impact, it is generally best not to conduct them more than once per week.

Agility/Plyometrics Workouts: You may choose to conduct dedicated agility or plyometrics workouts. It is also possible to combine these workouts with speed workouts, strength training or circuit training. Shorter workouts will help develop quickness while longer workouts will build more strength and endurance. Each workout will usually consist of several sets of plyometric or agility drills with rest in between each set.

Obstacle Course: If you have access to an obstacle course, it is useful to conduct obstacle course training as often as possible. It can also be useful to integrate obstacles into other workouts and practice negotiating obstacles in a variety of conditions. For example, when conducting a three mile tempo run, the challenge can be increased by conducting the run near the obstacle course and negotiating an obstacle after each mile. You can also practice negotiating obstacles when your muscles are tired from a strength training or swimming workout.

Ruck Workouts: Ruck workouts can be critical for the operational requirements of some units. Rucking is great exercises but it is also very taxing on the body. Therefore, it is generally best not to conduct ruck workouts more than once per week. It is also useful to slowly build up the ruck weight and movement distance to avoid injury.

Stick and Martial Arts Workouts: Stick training and martial arts workouts are easy to conduct and help build a variety of physical attributes. You can conduct stick drills over and over at a slower speed to build endurance, or conduct stick intervals at maximum speed to build quickness. If you have martial arts experience you can also incorporate bag workouts or grappling with a partner into your martial arts routine.

Traditional Swimming Workouts: If you are not part of a maritime unit, traditional swimming workouts might provide an effective, low-impact cross-training option. Such workouts are similar to running workouts and might consist of a long distance swim, a shorter speed swim or a series of intervals. If you are part of a maritime unit, you will probably require more specialized swim workouts.

Continuous Tally Workouts: Continuous tally workouts involve attempting to achieve the highest tally of repetitions, distance or exertion over the course of one day. For example, you might conduct a set number of push-ups every hour throughout the day, attempting to rack up the maximum number over the course of the day. Another example would be taking 5-15 minute breaks at the office and running up and down the stairs as many times as possible over the course of the day. Continuous tally workouts can be very effective, particularly for sustaining your fitness level when time and resources are limited. They can also prove a useful addition when conducted in the gaps between dedicated workout periods.

Specialized Maritime and Mountain Training: Detailed discussion of maritime or mountain fitness training is beyond the scope of this book. However, if you are part of a maritime or mountain unit, a large portion of your physical training will likely consist of advanced water or mountain fitness workouts.

Fitness Program Design: The Special Tactics Approach

While Special Tactics believes fitness routines must remain flexible to adjust to mission requirements, Special Tactics has developed its own approach to program design that could prove useful to a wide variety of tactical professionals. The approach is flexible and leaves a great deal of room for modification and adjustment based on mission requirements. The approach can also incorporate almost any selection of exercises or workout routines based on personal preferences. Remember, the Special Tactics approach is still only one approach to combat fitness and may not be the best fit for everyone or every unit. The core concepts explained in this book can be applied to any fitness program, not just a program based on the Special Tactics approach. The main tenants of the approach are as follows.

Program Structure: The Special Tactics program is built around a single, extended, high-intensity workout per week designed to push you to the limits of your capability in as many areas as possible. Ideally this "big workout" should last at least four hours but could be longer than eight hours depending on mission requirements. The remainder of the week consists of shorter, lower impact, targeted workouts intended to enhance and refine your athletic ability in the most efficient way possible. In addition, the program calls for slowly increasing the frequency and volume of continuous tally workouts (see previous section) in order to slowly expand your baseline capacity for work and exertion.

Big Workout Concept: The logic behind the "big workout" concept is that training should not necessarily revolve around the operational requirements that are the most common or likely, but should rather prepare you for the worst-case scenario that might get you killed, even if that scenario is less likely to occur. Preparing for the "fight gone bad" may seem like a waste of time until you find yourself in a bad situation and your physical abilities fall short. You may have to sprint to the extraction point after hiking for days through the mountains carrying casualties. You might have to overpower a criminal when you haven't slept and are exhausted from chasing him up multiple flights of stairs. The big workout is not simply about endurance; it is about being able to drag a heavy object when you are tired from sprinting or sprint when you are tired from dragging a heavy object. It is about finding ways to summon up explosive speed and strength when you have been hiking all day to the objective, then having the endurance to hike your way back while remaining prepared to fight a battle anywhere along the way. The concept behind the big workout is to prepare yourself for these types of scenarios.

Combat Performance Evaluations: The combat performance evaluation (discussed in the third chapter) is not technically part of your fitness program, but is rather the foundation for all of your training activities. However, conducting frequent combat performance evaluations is critical for employing the Special Tactics approach to combat fitness. The big workout is indeed a "workout," not a simulation of actual combat. The combat performance evaluation is still physically demanding but goes beyond fitness, attempting to cover as many tactical skills and tasks as possible. Also, unlike the big workout, the combat performance evaluation does not need to be long, it just has to be challenging and realistic. As discussed earlier, it is ideal to conduct at least one short combat performance evaluation per week and it is not necessary to plan it around your other workouts, since it can be useful to test combat performance in various levels of fatigue or soreness.

Low-Impact Workouts: There is logic behind the concept of "train as you fight," but given the intensity and danger associated with real fighting, training as you fight will likely lead to injury and physical breakdown. The purpose behind the big workout and combat performance evaluation is to place the most taxing, realistic and highest impact activities on only one or two days per week, freeing up the remaining days for lower-impact workouts designed to achieve the maximum increase in actual physical ability. These workouts are not designed to punish or toughen the body but instead to improve strength, speed and endurance while minimizing the chances of injury. In short, you punish your body one or two-days each week, and pamper it for the remaining five days. For these low-impact workouts, it is better to run with no gear on a rubberized track with good running shoes, or deadlift light weight slowly with perfect form, than it is to hike up a mountain in the rain carrying a sandbag. Save that for the big workout or combat performance evaluation. If you train as you fight every day, you will just break yourself down faster.

Continuous Tally Training for Capacity Expansion: Continuous tally training involves working out continuously, all day, in an attempt to achieve the maximum tally of a given exercise or exertion (see the previous section for details). There are countless ways to weave continuous tally training into your daily routine. The purpose of continuous tally training is to expand your capacity for work and help you create a new baseline or new "normal" for physical exertion. If you were to spend several weeks lying in bed, the daily routine you consider "normal" at the moment might prove taxing. Simply walking around all day or climbing stairs might prove taxing or leave you sore the next day. However, because you have not spent the past few weeks lying in bed but instead have conducted the same activities every day, they have become normal. They are part of your baseline exertion and they do not affect your ability to put forth additional exertion beyond the baseline. Continuous tally training simply expands your baseline and forms habits of increasing physical exertion over time.

Flexibility and Sustainment: One of the biggest problems that tactical athletes face is the difficulty of maintianing physical fitness in the midst of unpredictable operational demands and work schedules. One of the advantages of combining the various elements explained above is that it is very easy to scale up or scale down the fitness program based on unpredictable schedule changes. If necessary, you can eliminate the low-intensity workouts and sustain your existing fitness level or even make progress with only the daily continuous tally training and one big workout per week. If demands grow even higher, you can maintain your fitness level with either the continuous tally training or the single big workout alone. When your schedule changes and you have more available time for training, you can scale up your program by adding more low-intensity workouts.

Train Beyond Operational Demands: By focusing on the worst-case scenario with the big workout, and expanding your baseline capacity with your continuous tally training, you are training beyond your operational demands. Training beyond your operational demands aims to make operational tasks easy when they arrive. To offer an analogy, if you train to bench-press 225 lbs., you may achieve your goal but benching that weight will likely prove difficult. However, if you train to bench-press 265 lbs. and achieve your goal, 265 lbs. may feel heavy but 225 lbs. will feel like nothing. This same concept applies to training beyond the likely demands of real-world operations. When the physical demands of an operation are easy to handle, that means you will be able to focus maximum energy and attention on the enemy and the fight at hand without being distracted by physical discomfort, pain or fatigue.

FITNESS PROGRAM DESIGN EXAMPLES

Overview

Below is an example of a complete fitness program design, based on the Special Tactics approach just described. This is only one example of a program designed using Special Tactics approach and it is possible to design an infinite variety of programs either using the Special Tactics approach or other fitness philosophies. The main purpose of this section is not to provide you with pre-formatted workouts but instead to offer examples that you can use as a reference when designing your own custom program.

In some cases, you might want to design your program from scratch or in other cases you can use your existing workout as a starting point. You can also use the example workouts that follow as a starting point and modify them as needed to fit your own requirements. The example workouts are balanced routines that attempt to place relatively equal empahsis on strength, speed, endurance etc. To adjust the routines for your own purposes, you can simply adjust or replace the individual workouts. For example, if your mission requirements places a greater emphasis on strength, you can remove some of the long runs or endurance workouts and replace them with strength workouts.

It is also important to note that the following example workouts were constructed using only the exercises covered in this book, along with some well-known exercises that require little explanation. Therefore, when you construct your own custom program, you will have a much wider selection of exercises to choose from. Also, in all of the example workouts, Sunday is considered a rest day and no activity is displayed for Sunday.

Finally, in all of the following programs, it is possible to switch the morning and evening workouts based on schedule restrictions. Each program offers a different intensity level. It is important to remember that higher-intensity programs are not necessarily more "advanced" but you should rather adjust the intensity of your program based on operational requirements, time available and your periodization plan. As already explained, the Special Tactics approach is designed so you can scale down your program to only one "big workout" per week under extreme circumstances.

FITNESS PROGRAM DESIGN EXAMPLES

High-Intensity Balanced Program (1 of 2)

	MONDAY	TUESDAY	WEDNESDAY
MORNING	15 min Stick Training Running Drills 6 x 100m Sprints (Full recovery) Contrast shower	Dynamic Stretch Warmup Power Plyometrics • Box Drop (10-10-10) • Box Jump (10-10-10) • Linear Hops (10-10-10 • Diagonal Hops (10-10-10) Contrast shower	15 min Stick Training 4 x 50m Speed Swim Contrast shower
	BREAKFAST: Combination of 8-12 oz. of TURKEY, chicken or fish with rice, potato or pasta		
EVENING	Dynamic Stretch Warmup Running Drills 3-Mile Tempo Run Recovery: Static stretch in sauna/whirlpool, foam roller, topical analgesic	Lower Body Strength Workout • 12 min Cardio Warmup • Deadlift (10-10-10) • Step-up (10-10-10) • Posterior Lunge (10-10-10) • 4-Way Hip (10-10-10 Each way) • Leg Extension (10-10-10) • Leg Curl (10-10-10) • Calf Extension (10-10-10) • Uni-Lateral Abs (Max-Max-Max) Recovery: Static stretch, 20 min ice bath, topical analgesic	Upper Body Strength Workout • 12 min Cardio Warmup • Weighted Pull-Up (4-4-4) • Bench Press (10-10-10) • One-Arm Row (10-10-10) • One-Arm Overhead Press (10-10-10) • Cable Row (10-10-10) • Bicep and Tricep (choice) • Leg Press (1 set light weight) Recovery: Static stretch in sauna/whirlpool, foam roller, topical analgesic
ALL DAY	Push-ups, flutter kicks, grip, balance board and stairs All day fruit/vegetable smoothie	Push-ups, flutter kicks, grip, balance board and stairs All day fruit/vegetable smoothie	Push-ups, flutter kicks, grip, balance board and stairs All day fruit/vegetable smoothie
	DINNER: Combination of 12-16 oz. of beef or lamb with rice, potato or pasta		

FITNESS PROGRAM DESIGN EXAMPLES

High-Intensity Balanced Program (2 of 2)

	THURSDAY	FRIDAY	SATURDAY
MORNING	Dynamic Stretch Warmup Speed/Agility Ladder (6 x Each Drill) Contrast shower	15 min Stick Training Contrast shower	
	BREAKFAST: Combination of 8-12 oz. of TURKEY, chicken or fish with rice, potato or pasta		
EVENING	Dynamic Stretch Warmup Running Drills Hill Intervals: 4 x 400m (Full recovery) Recovery: Static stretch, 20 min ice bath, topical analgesic	Dynamic Stretch Warmup Running Drills Speed Plyometrics • Six-Count (30-30-30) • Lateral Box Hops (30-30-30) Climbing wall (30-60 min) Sports (30-120 min) Recovery: Static stretch in sauna/whirlpool, foam roller, topical analgesic	**BIG WORKOUT (No break between events)** Dynamic Stretch Warmup Timed Obstacle Course 3-Part Run (10 miles total) • 3-Mile Tempo Run • Pyramid Intervals: 200-400-600-800-1K-800-600-400 (2 min rest) • 4-Mile Distance Run 800m Swim Total Body Strength Circuit (x 3) • Pull-Ups (Max) • Deadlift (10) • Incline Bench (10) • One-Arm Row (10) • One-Arm Overhead Press (10) • Reverse Wood-Chopper (20) 1-Hour Stick Training (Constant movemet) Hill Ruck (Light-Medium weight, push to physical limit) Timed Obstacle Course Recovery: 25 min ice bath, topical analgesic
ALL DAY	Push-ups, flutter kicks, grip, balance board and stairs All day fruit/vegetable smoothie	Push-ups, flutter kicks, grip, balance board and stairs All day fruit/vegetable smoothie	
	DINNER: Combination of 12-16 oz. of beef or lamb with rice, potato or pasta		

FITNESS PROGRAM DESIGN EXAMPLES

Medium-Intensity Balanced Program (1 of 2)

	MONDAY	TUESDAY	WEDNESDAY
MORNING	15 min Stick Training Contrast shower	Dynamic Stretch Warmup Power Plyometrics • Box Drop (10-10-10) • Box Jump (10-10-10) • Linear Hops (10-10-10) • Diagonal Hops (10-10-10) Contrast shower	15 min Stick Training Contrast shower
	BBREAKFAST: Combination of 8-12 oz. of TURKEY, chicken or fish with rice, potato or pasta		
EVENING	Dynamic Stretch Warmup Running Drills Speed Intervals: 4 x 400m (Full recovery) Recovery: Static stretch, 20 min ice bath, topical analgesic	Upper Body Strength Workout • 12 min Cardio Warmup • Weighted Pull-Up (4-4-4) • Bench Press (10-10-10) • One-Arm Row (10-10-10) • One-Arm Overhead Press (10-10-10) • Cable Row (10-10-10) • Bicep and Tricep (choice) • Leg Press (1 set light weight) • Uni-Lateral Abs (Max-Max-Max) Recovery: Static stretch in sauna/whirlpool, foam roller, topical analgesic	Dynamic Stretch Warmup Running Drills 3-Mile Tempo Run Recovery: Static stretch in sauna/whirlpool, foam roller, topical analgesic
ALL DAY	Push-ups, flutter kicks, grip, balance board and stairs All day fruit/vegetable smoothie	Push-ups, flutter kicks, grip, balance board and stairs All day fruit/vegetable smoothie	Push-ups, flutter kicks, grip, balance board and stairs All day fruit/vegetable smoothie
	DINNER: Combination of 12-16 oz. of beef or lamb with rice, potato or pasta		

FITNESS PROGRAM DESIGN EXAMPLES

Medium-Intensity Balanced Program (2 of 2)

	THURSDAY	FRIDAY	SATURDAY
MORNING	4 x 50m Speed Swim Contrast shower	15 min Stick Training Contrast shower	
BREAKFAST: Combination of 8-12 oz. of TURKEY, chicken or fish with rice, potato or pasta			
EVENING	Lower Body Strength Workout • 12 min Cardio Warmup • Deadlift (10-10-10) • Step-up (10-10-10) • Posterior Lunge (10-10-10) • 4-Way Hip (10-10-10 Each way) • Leg Extension (10-10-10) • Leg Curl (10-10-10) • Calf Extension (10-10-10) • Uni-Lateral Abs (Max-Max-Max) Recovery: Static stretch, 20 min ice bath, topical analgesic	Dynamic Stretch Warmup Running Drills Speed Plyometrics • Six-Count (30-30-30) • Lateral Box Hops (30-30-30) Climbing wall (30-60 min) Sports (30-120 min) Recovery: Static stretch in sauna/whirlpool, foam roller, topical analgesic	**BIG WORKOUT (No break between events)** Dynamic Stretch Warmup Timed Obstacle Course 3-Part Run (10 miles total) • 3-Mile Tempo Run • Pyramid Intervals: 200-400-600-800-1K-800-600-400 (2 min rest) • 4-Mile Distance Run 800m Swim Total Body Strength Circuit (x 3) • Pull-Ups (Max) • Deadlift (10) • Incline Bench (10) • One-Arm Row (10) • One-Arm Overhead Press (10) • Reverse Wood-Chopper (20) • Bi-Lateral Abs (Max-Max-Max) Timed Obstacle Course Recovery: 25 min ice bath, topical analgesic
ALL DAY	Push-ups, flutter kicks, grip, balance board and stairs All day fruit/vegetable smoothie	Push-ups, flutter kicks, grip, balance board and stairs All day fruit/vegetable smoothie	
DINNER: Combination of 12-16 oz. of beef or lamb with rice, potato or pasta			

FITNESS PROGRAM DESIGN EXAMPLES

Lighter-Intensity Balanced Program (1 of 2)

	MONDAY	TUESDAY	WEDNESDAY
MORNING	15 min Stick Training Contrast shower	15 min Stick Training Contrast shower	15 min Stick Training Contrast shower
BREAKFAST: Combination of 8-12 oz. of TURKEY, chicken or fish with rice, potato or pasta			
EVENING	Dynamic Stretch Warmup Running Drills Speed Intervals: 4 x 200 (Full recovery) Recovery: Static stretch, 20 min ice bath, topical analgesic	Upper Body Strength Workout • 12 min Cardio Warmup • Weighted Pull-Up (4-4-4) • Bench Press (10-10-10) • One-Arm Row (10-10-10) • One-Arm Overhead Press (10-10-10) • Bicep and Tricep (choice) • Leg Press (1 set light weight) • Uni-Lateral Abs (Max-Max-Max) Recovery: Static stretch in sauna/whirlpool, foam roller, topical analgesic	Dynamic Stretch Warmup Running Drills 3-Mile Tempo Run Recovery: Static stretch in sauna/whirlpool, foam roller, topical analgesic
ALL DAY	Push-ups, flutter kicks, grip, balance board and stairs All day fruit/vegetable smoothie	Push-ups, flutter kicks, grip, balance board and stairs All day fruit/vegetable smoothie	Push-ups, flutter kicks, grip, balance board and stairs All day fruit/vegetable smoothie
DINNER: Combination of 12-16 oz. of beef or lamb with rice, potato or pasta			

FITNESS PROGRAM DESIGN EXAMPLES

Lighter-Intensity Balanced Program (2 of 2)

	THURSDAY	FRIDAY	SATURDAY
MORNING	15 min Stick Training Contrast shower	15 min Stick Training Contrast shower	
	BREAKFAST: Combination of 8-12 oz. of TURKEY, chicken or fish with rice, potato or pasta		
EVENING	Lower Body Strength Workout • 12 min Cardio Warmup • Step-up (10-10-10) • Posterior Lunge (10-10-10) • 4-Way Hip (10-10-10 Each way) • Calf Extension (10-10-10) • Uni-Lateral Abs (Max-Max-Max) Recovery: Static stretch, 20 min ice bath, topical analgesic	Dynamic Stretch Warmup Climbing wall or Sports (30-60 min) Recovery: Static stretch in sauna/whirlpool, foam roller, topical analgesic	**BIG WORKOUT (No break between events)** Dynamic Stretch Warmup Timed Obstacle Course 3-Part Run (10 miles total) • 3-Mile Tempo Run • Pyramid Intervals: 200-400-600-800-1K-800-600-400 (2 min rest) • 4-Mile Distance Run 800m Swim Total Body Strength Circuit (x 3) • Pull-Ups (Max) • Deadlift (10) • Incline Bench (10) • One-Arm Row (10) • One-Arm Overhead Press (10) • Reverse Wood-Chopper (20) • Bi-Lateral Abs (Max-Max-Max) Timed Obstacle Course Recovery: 25 min ice bath, topical analgesic
ALL DAY	Push-ups, flutter kicks, grip, balance board and stairs All day fruit/vegetable smoothie	Push-ups, flutter kicks, grip, balance board and stairs All day fruit/vegetable smoothie	
	DINNER: Combination of 12-16 oz. of beef or lamb with rice, potato or pasta		

FITNESS PROGRAM DESIGN EXAMPLES

Day-On-Day-Off Balanced Program (1 of 2)

	MONDAY	TUESDAY	WEDNESDAY
MORNING		15 min Stick Training Dynamic Stretch Warmup Running Drills Speed Intervals: 4 x 200 (Full recovery) Contrast shower	
	BBREAKFAST: Combination of 8-12 oz. of TURKEY, chicken or fish with rice, potato or pasta		
EVENING	Climbing wall or Sports (30-60 min) Recovery: Static stretch in sauna/whirlpool, foam roller, topical analgesic	Upper Body Strength Workout • 12 min Cardio Warmup • Weighted Pull-Up (4-4-4) • Bench Press (10-10-10) • One-Arm Row (10-10-10) • One-Arm Overhead Press (10-10-10) • Cable Row (10-10-10) • Bicep and Tricep (choice) • Leg Press (1 set light weight) • Uni-Lateral Abs (Max-Max-Max) Recovery: Static stretch in sauna/whirlpool, foam roller, topical analgesic	
ALL DAY	All day fruit/vegetable smoothie	Push-ups, flutter kicks, grip, balance board and stairs All day fruit/vegetable smoothie	All day fruit/vegetable smoothie
	DINNER: Combination of 12-16 oz. of beef or lamb with rice, potato or pasta		

FITNESS PROGRAM DESIGN EXAMPLES

Day-On-Day-Off Balanced Program (2 of 2)

	THURSDAY	FRIDAY	SATURDAY
MORNING	15 min Stick Training Dynamic Stretch Warmup Running Drills 3-Mile Tempo Run Contrast shower		
	BREAKFAST: Combination of 8-12 oz. of TURKEY, chicken or fish with rice, potato or pasta		
EVENING	Lower Body Strength Workout • 12 min Cardio Warmup • Deadlift (10-10-10) • Step-up (10-10-10) • Posterior Lunge (10-10-10) • 4-Way Hip (10-10-10 Each way) • Leg Extension (10-10-10) • Leg Curl (10-10-10) • Calf Extension (10-10-10) • Uni-Lateral Abs (Max-Max-Max) Recovery: Static stretch, 20 min ice bath, topical analgesic		**BIG WORKOUT (No break between events)** Dynamic Stretch Warmup Timed Obstacle Course 3-Part Run (10 miles total) • 3-Mile Tempo Run • Pyramid Intervals: 200-400-600-800-1K-800-600-400 (2 min rest) • 4-Mile Distance Run 800m Swim Total Body Strength Circuit (x 3) • Pull-Ups (Max) • Deadlift (10) • Incline Bench (10) • One-Arm Row (10) • One-Arm Overhead Press (10) • Reverse Wood-Chopper (20) • Bi-Lateral Abs (Max-Max-Max) Timed Obstacle Course Recovery: 25 min ice bath, topical analgesic
ALL DAY	Push-ups, flutter kicks, grip, balance board and stairs All day fruit/vegetable smoothie	All day fruit/vegetable smoothie	
	DINNER: Combination of 12-16 oz. of beef or lamb with rice, potato or pasta		

FITNESS PROGRAM DESIGN EXAMPLES

Minimized Balanced Program (1 of 2)

	MONDAY	TUESDAY	WEDNESDAY
MORNING	15 min Stick Training (optional) Static stretch (optional) Contrast shower (optional)	15 min Stick Training (optional) Static stretch (optional) Contrast shower (optional)	15 min Stick Training (optional) Static stretch (optional) Contrast shower (optional)
BREAKFAST: Combination of 8-12 oz. of TURKEY, chicken or fish with rice, potato or pasta			
EVENING			
ALL DAY	Push-ups, flutter kicks, grip, balance board and stairs All day fruit/vegetable smoothie	Push-ups, flutter kicks, grip, balance board and stairs All day fruit/vegetable smoothie	Push-ups, flutter kicks, grip, balance board and stairs All day fruit/vegetable smoothie
DINNER: Combination of 12-16 oz. of beef or lamb with rice, potato or pasta			

FITNESS PROGRAM DESIGN EXAMPLES

Minimized Balanced Program (2 of 2)

	THURSDAY	FRIDAY	SATURDAY
MORNING	15 min Stick Training (optional) Static stretch (optional) Contrast shower (optional)	15 min Stick Training (optional) Static stretch (optional) Contrast shower (optional)	
	BREAKFAST: Combination of 8-12 oz. of TURKEY, chicken or fish with rice, potato or pasta		
EVENING			**BIG WORKOUT (No break between events)** Dynamic Stretch Warmup Timed Obstacle Course 3-Part Run (10 miles total) • 3-Mile Tempo Run • Pyramid Intervals: 200-400-600-800-1K-800-600-400 (2 min rest) • 4-Mile Distance Run 800m Swim Total Body Strength Circuit (x 3) • Pull-Ups (Max) • Deadlift (10) • Incline Bench (10) • One-Arm Row (10) • One-Arm Overhead Press (10) • Reverse Wood-Chopper (20) • Bi-Lateral Abs (Max-Max-Max) Timed Obstacle Course Recovery: 25 min ice bath, topical analgesic
ALL DAY	Push-ups, flutter kicks, grip, balance board and stairs All day fruit/vegetable smoothie	Push-ups, flutter kicks, grip, balance board and stairs All day fruit/vegetable smoothie	
	DINNER: Combination of 12-16 oz. of beef or lamb with rice, potato or pasta		

PROGRAM DESIGN AND TRACKING
Performance Tracking Techniques

Some level of performance or progress tracking is an essential component of any combat fitness or athletic fitness program. Without the ability to measure progress or performance, it is impossible to know whether a fitness program is working or not. While some form of performance tracking is critical, it is not necessary to spend excessive time or energy on the tracking process. While detailed and complex tracking systems can be useful, it is often possible to achieve nearly equal results with much more simple and streamlined tracking systems. For example, simply keeping a record of run times and distances, exercise weights and repetitions over time will give you a clear indication of progress.

This section provides a number of general suggestions and concepts that might help you track your combat fitness performance. In addition, this section discusses the design and incorporation of more traditional physical fitness tests into your training program. Finally, the most important reason for measuring performance is so you can adjust and improve your program over time. Therefore, the end of this section provides suggestions for how to use the data you collect to drive improvements to your fitness program.

As with fitness program design, performance tracking is not just for combat units. It is possible to conduct the same type of performance tracking as an individual and to use that performance data to greatly improve your rate of progress. However, as an individual, the performance tracking process can often be simpler and more streamlined.

Performance Tracking Fundamentals

There are an unlimited number of methods and approaches to performance tracking and you should choose the approach that works the best for you. As with the combat fitness program itself, you may also want to adjust and improve your tracking procedures over time. Below are several critical fundamentals to keep in mind when tracking performance.

Fitness Performance vs. Combat Performance: It is important to remember that just because your fitness performance is improving, that does not mean that your combat performance is improving. For example, if you are making great progress in long distance running, but long distance running has few applications to your actual operational requirements, your combat performance will increase only marginally at best. Therefore, the key is to align your fitness program with your operational requirements, then establish a correlation between fitness performance and combat performance.

Fitness to Combat Correlation: It does not take advanced mathematics or tracking systems to identify correlations between fitness performance and combat performance. All you must do is conduct an adequately wide selection of fitness tests on each member of your unit, and then design one or more realistic combat performance evaluations (see the third chapter) that replicate your real-world mission requirements as accurately as possible. Even without looking at the data, it will be quite easy to see what physical attributes are the best fit for your mission requirements. If the stronger and bulkier members of your unit are winded, struggling and falling behind, then strength and bulk are not ideal attributes for your mission. However, if the smaller, more wiry unit members are getting overwhelmed and overpowered, then maybe your mission places a greater demand on size and strength. The process is simple, design a test that replicates real mission conditions and then identify which physical attributes prove the most useful. While it is possible to learn a lot just through observation, you can go into greater detail by comparing charts of graphs of performance data as well.

Identify Key Fitness Performance Metrics: Once you have established a correlation between certain physical attributes and the chances of mission success, you can then identify specific fitness metrics that have a high correlation with combat performance. These are the best metrics to focus on when evaluating the fitness progress of unit members and measuring the effectiveness of your combat fitness program. Some examples of common fitness metrics might include runing times/speed, movement distances, lifting weights, max exercise repetitions circuit completion times, flexibility measurements and heart rates during various activities.

Competitions and Leaderboards: Holding competitions within the unit is one of the best ways to increase motivation and performance. Ideally, every physical activity should also be a competition and all competitors should strive to win. If direct competition is not possible, you can post "leaderboards" around the unit that display the top 5 or 10 unit members in a given exercise or skill. You can also have a board that displays the all-time unit records. This will encourage all unit members to strive to be the best and take pride in personal achievement. Ideally, it is good for each level of command to have a separate set of leaderboards, so while a company or battalion will have their own leaderboards, subordinate platoons and squads will also have their own.

Performance Tracking Technology: One of the biggest problems with performance tracking is that it takes time and energy away from actual training. It is always important to ensure that you do not get so consumed with performance tracking that you spend more time studying data than you do working out. New performance tracking technologies, especially wearable technologies, have made performance tracking and analysis much easier. Such technologies could prove beneficial for tactical athletes and help save a great deal of time and effort.

Fitness Testing and Combat Performance Evaluations

As discussed in the previous section, it is very important to differentiate between fitness performance and combat performance. While the fundamental concept of the performance tracking model just described calls for finding a correlation between fitness performance and combat performance, fitness performance tracking can never replace the combat performance evaluation described at the beginning of this book. Below are several points on how to best integrate your fitness program with combat performance evaluations.

The Physical Fitness Test Cycle: Reviewing the suggestions in this book to this point, you might notice that there is no discussion of a "physical fitness test," in the traditional sense. Physical fitness tests in military or tactical units often prove problematic and go through a never-ending cycle from "practical to tactical," and back again. Fitness tests will start off as simple tests of strength, speed and endurance. However, the argument will undoubtedly come up that the test does not measure "tactical fitness." The test will then change to a long, resource intensive, complicated set of events designed to replicate combat conditions but that are frequently difficult to score or quantify. After a while, people become frustrated about the time, resources and complexity of the tactical fitness tests and switch back to a practical test. The cycle then continues. The frequently overlooked solution lies in the concept of the combat performance evaluation described at the beginning of this book.

Combat Performance Evaluation: The reason why it is difficult or impossible to create a fitness test that replicates combat conditions is for two main reasons. First, combat is not just about fitness but instead involves the integration of many different abilities and skills at once in a high-stress environment. Second, the demands of combat are so broad and mission-dependent that they could never be captured in a single, codified test. The combat performance evaluation solves both of these problems since it is not only a fitness test but a test of multiple combat abilities at once and units are free to plan, execute and modify their own combat performance evaluations as often as necessary to meet mission requirements. There is only so much time for evaluations and tests, so lumping multiple tests into one saves time and energy. In the end, the only test that really matters is the one that answers the question, "can you do your job?" That is the purpose the combat performance evaluation.

Combat Performance Evaluation Results: Combat performance evaluation results are difficult to measure and quantify. Some aspects of an evaluation can be recorded and scored (like speed of movement, shooting accuracy etc.) but others require more detailed evaluation. The best way to accomplish this is to film each combat performance evaluation and then review the video afterwards as a unit, much like how a sports team analyzes film from the last game. There are no fixed formulas for evaluating or scoring combat performance evaluations so it is best to use your common sense, measuring what can be measured and using analytical thinking to examine the rest.

Options for "Fitness Only" Tests: While the most operationally useful test is the combat performance evaluation, some units may want to incorporate a more traditional physical fitness test into their training program. If you are already conducting a combat performance test, it is not necessary to expend time and resources to make the fitness test overly "combat focused." You are already measuring combat ability through the combat performance evaluation. Therefore, the best fitness tests are often simple and are not resource intensive. As long as you remember that the results of the fitness test are not an indication of actual combat performance, there is nothing wrong with having a fitness test that is simpler and more traditional.

Program Modification and Optimization

The most important reason for measuring performance is so you can adjust and improve your program over time. You might start out with one physical fitness program but subsequent data and evaluations (both fitness and combat focused) may reveal that your program is not achieving the desired results for your specific mission set. After you implement changes to your program, you can go back and see if the changes caused an improvement in results or not. This process does not have to be overly complicated but is possibly one of the most critical components of an effective combat fitness program. What follows are a few guidelines for using performance data to modify your fitness program.

Implement Changes in Isolation When Possible: Once you have established effective performance tracking metrics, it is best to implement changes to your fitness program one at a time. That way you can see the effect that each change has on performance. The same principles apply to changes in nutrition programs or recovery programs etc. If you implement multiple changes at one time and your performance is increasing, you cannot be sure which change is most responsible for the positive results.

Give Changes Time to Take Effect: If you implement a change to your fitness program, you may not be able to identify results right away. Therefore, give changes time to take effect and look for measurable changes in performance data over time. This will also reduce the possibility that some other, uncontrolled variables might be responsible for changes in performance data in the short term. Essentially, make an effort to confirm the real effects of a change before deciding to keep it or discard it.

Control Groups and Experimental Groups: In larger units with adequate time and resources, it might prove beneficial to conduct actual "fitness experiments" using a scientific approach. One group (the experimental group) will implement a change to the fitness program while the other group (the control group) does not implement any change. You can then measure differences in performance results between the control group and the experimental group.

CONCLUSION
A Habit of Adaptation

The process of evaluation and adaptation described in this book is a small-scale rehearsal for what will make you effective in real combat operations. Possibly the most universal trait of skilled fighters and effective combat units is that they constantly evaluate their performance and use that information to improve, while adapting to the threat and the operating environment. The mindset described in this book for creating the optimum combat fitness program is the same mindset that will lead to success in combat and victory on the battlefield.

It is important to remember once again that this book is about the "bigger picture" when it comes to combat fitness. The individual exercises and routines described in this book are just examples or suggestions. We strongly encourage you not to simply accept everything in this book and apply it directly to your own program. Instead, we suggest you take the concepts from this book and use them to build the ideal combat fitness program for you, based on what has worked for you in the past and what can help you succeed in the future.

If you have any questions, suggestions, positive or negative feedback regarding this manual, the Special Tactics staff encourages you to contact us on our website at ***www.SpecialTactics.me***. We look forward to hearing from you and we hope that you found this combat fitness manual worthwhile.